What Others Are Saying...

"This important and enjoyable book is loaded with great ideas you can use to achieve the financial independence you deserve."

Brian Tracy, Author, Million Dollar Habits

"Thanks for taking a boring subject and making it useful and entertaining to read. **How to be Rich** *gave me money tips I can easily use today to sleep better at night."*

Lori Speer, P.E., Civil Engineer, Wife & Mother

"This book is written straight from the heart, you can learn both the emotional and technical sides of how to stop your money anxieties."

Linda Leitz, CFP', EA, Author,
We Need to Talk: Money and Kids After Divorce

"Accessible, authentic & authoritative: Chuck has created a personal finance book that offers to the masses what many in the financial industry have not yet learned. He speaks to the pervasive force that money is in our lives driven by our individual values, goals & emotions."

Nathan G. Gehring, CFP',
Founder Couples Financial Planning, LLC

"Finally, a book about money for busy people with work, life, and kids. The story had me turning the pages so fast I didn't even realize I was learning along the way."

Rob Morris, Police Sergeant & Father

What Others Are Saying...

"Chuck gets it! Discipline is the key that separates those who succeed from those who fail. Financial freedom is one-tenth having a plan and nine-tenths sticking to the plan. Do you have what it takes to be rich?"

Rick A. Ferri, CFA, Author,

All About Asset Allocation

"This isn't the same old information that you've seen in other personal finance books. This is a completely different approach that is both simple and fun to read. If you want to take your finances and your relationship with money to the next level, read this book."

Russ Thornton, Vice President,

Wealthcare Capital Management

"This book is amazing. Chuck blends an impressive ability as a storyteller with his extensive experience as a financial planner to draw the reader into a real-to-life story that subtly gives them financial education and guidance for their own lives. I highly recommend this book to anyone who wants to improve their financial situation, but doesn't know where to start. The book is a quick read. You will learn a lot, and have fun doing it."

John Marx, Founder,

The Law Enforcement Survival Institute

STOP! Before You Proceed

As a reader of this book, you are entitled to FREE advanced training. Before you proceed, visit www.NoMoreMoneyWorry.com and claim your free bonuses now before you get distracted.

The book that you hold in your hands is only the beginning. There is a ton of FREE training available only to readers of this book. Using passwords hidden in this book, you can access some very powerful training that will take you and your finances to the next level.

Visit: www.NoMoreMoneyWorry.com

Disclaimer

This book is designed to provide information on personal finance. It is sold with the understanding that in the context of this book, the author and/or publisher are not able to provide legal, accounting or other personal financial advice. If legal or other expert assistance is required, the services of a competent attorney, accountant, or Fee-Only personal financial advisor should be sought.

It is not the purpose of this book to reprint all the information that is otherwise available to authors and/or publishers, but instead to complement, amplify, and supplement other texts. The reader is urged to read all the available material, learn as much as possible about personal finance, and tailor the information to individual needs.

This book is not a get-rich-quick scheme. Anyone who decides to organize their personal finances must expect to invest a lot of time and effort into it. Some people are more successful than others at arranging their finances to create the lifestyle they desire, but it usually is a direct result of the amount of effort they put into it.

Every effort has been made to make this book as complete and accurate as possible. However, there may be mistakes, both typographical and in content. Therefore, this text should be used only as a general guide and not as the ultimate source of personal finance information. Furthermore, this manual contains information on personal finance that is current only up to the printing date.

The purpose of this book is to educate and entertain. The author and publisher shall have neither liability nor responsibility to any person or entity with respect to any loss or damage caused, or alleged to have been caused, directly or indirectly, by the information contained in this book.

If you do not wish to be bound by the above, you may return this book for a full refund.

HOW to be Rich

The couple's guide to a rich life
WITHOUT WORRYING
ABOUT MONEY

CHUCK J. RYLANT, MBA, CFP®

PERFECT LIFE PUBLISHING

ISBN 978-0-9839637-0-7
Library of Congress Control Number: 2011915806

Published by:
Perfect Life Publishing
793 Foothill Boulevard, Suite 165
San Luis Obispo, CA 93405-1683

Cover and Interior Design:
Jerry & Michelle Dorris
Authorsupport.com

Contents

Richard and Janet's Story

Introduction

Nothing creates stress or anxiety within a family like money. Not having enough money can create real stress, but fear of not having enough can elicit the same or even greater fear than not actually having it at all.

The reality is that money is a tool to get the stuff we want and need. However, in our society money has also become a measure of self-worth and perceived happiness. We are surrounded by messages from our parents, friends, neighbors, coworkers, and the media that encourage these misguided feelings.

These complex emotions are what create most of the problems—fear, anger, resentment, and frustration—that revolve around money. However, most of the personal finance industry ignores these core feelings, and instead focuses on interest rates, stocks, bonds, and taxes.

Like money, these things are simply tools to get you where you want to be and are not the end goal. Happiness and fulfillment are the end goal for most of us, yet we often lose sight of that when dealing with our money.

I wrote this book on two different tracks. The first is the deep and complex emotional issues families struggle with because of money. The second is the nuts and bolts of financial planning that allow you to organize your money.

To get the most from this book, while you're enjoying the entertaining story line, keep in mind that the emotional issues are the most important part of the story. The financial planning tools are secondary to the emotional aspects. If you can learn from both messages, you will walk away from this book with a completely different perspective about money.

I didn't figure this out overnight. It took me a long time to discover what matters, and sadly, I think many people never learn it themselves. I first started learning about the world of money and investing at the ripe old age of eighteen when I studied investment magazines like they were textbooks. It wasn't until almost ten years later that I realized they were actually advertisements for underperforming and overpriced mutual funds.

It was also at eighteen that I invested my first $1,000 in mutual funds—a front-end-loaded technology fund that was a completely inappropriate investment for a kid, but an easy sale for a commissioned stockbroker, or otherwise said, a salesperson.

Years later, through lots of self-guided education in books and mistakes in the market, I figured out what was most important in personal finance. (This wasn't before a ridiculous stint when I thought I could be a day trader, picking individual stocks and even dabbling in IPOs.) Eventually, I received the formal education and financial planning credentials, an MBA degree, and tax training to be "qualified" to give personal financial planning advice. It wasn't until I had a wife, divorce, remarriage, stepchild, jobs, businesses, my own child, a deceased parent, and worked as a financial advisor with other real-world complicated families that I learned what really mattered.

That was when I learned about personal financial planning. I learned that people, including me, don't care about the highest performing mutual fund of the year, or the highest yielding CD, or the latest tax deduction. What you and I care about is enjoying life with our families without the money worries that plague most Americans. What we want is to live extraordinary lives. That's what this book is about—getting back to the basics about what you want and providing some basic money tools to help you get there.

Richard and Janet's Story

Surprise

On Richard and Janet's first anniversary, Valentine's Day, everything was going to be perfect.

Janet had planned the evening down to the last detail. Dinner out, check. Special dress, check. Big announcement? She wasn't so sure. She had something to tell him—something that had happened earlier than they planned. But she hoped Richard would be happy.

Ever since Richard had stuck up for her at that dive bar in Encino, they'd been inseparable. She relied on him for his strength and courage. Although she'd never imagined from her pampered upbringing that she'd marry a police officer, she felt safe with him. Their life together wasn't perfect, but whose was? Marriage had happened after a few years of dating, and they'd thought they'd have some time to enjoy life. Now, things would change again.

That afternoon, Janet swung into their disorganized rental in Ventura, California, boutique bags on her arm. She stalked past the mail pile on the dining room table with the tax statements and the credit card bills. After a glance at the bills, which were her job, she threw them back on the table. She ignored the tax information—Richard said he would take care of that this year. Maybe money was a little tight, but when wasn't it? Her pharmaceuticals sales job was mostly in the car and on the phone, so she could try to keep working, even after—well, she'd think about that later.

She went to the bedroom to rummage for the perfect earrings to go with her new dress. *At least it was on sale,* she thought. Shoes, however, had been trickier. She'd had to splurge a bit on the right high heels, but after all, this might be the last night she'd look this good for a long time—if ever. Richard would be picking her up for their dinner in Santa Barbara after work, and she wanted to look dazzling.

* * *

Janet wasn't the only one with a surprise. Richard looked forward to that night, too. He had great news—he finally got that promotion from police officer to detective on the narcotics squad. No more uniforms; no more squad cars. And, some more money, just in time, so he could go on the annual hunting trip with the guys—as long as no unexpected expenses came up.

Richard knew the dinner that night was important to Janet, so he tried to get out of work early. But the afternoon was destroyed with getting up to speed on a new case his team was investigating. There was a meth gang working out of San Diego, with the drugs coming over the border from Mexico. This was just the kind of case he'd be able to sink his teeth into. Before he knew it, he was in overtime.

Surprise

When he saw the clock, he winced. He had a flash image of Janet, standing in their living room, arms crossed and toe tapping. As much as he knew she loved him, she didn't like it when he was late. *Man,* he thought, *I'm in trouble.*

The Dinner

Richard rushed to the shower at the station to clean up and change. After he shaved, he decided to send Janet a text message saying he was on his way. Texting was always better when he wasn't sure how she'd respond. The reassuring "whoosh" sound let him know his message had been sent.

But as he unlocked the car door, his phone started chiming. He picked it up as he started to drive.

"You had to text me?" Janet said, without even a hello first. "Why didn't you call? Where are you?"

"On my way, sweetheart, I'm in the car."

"You're on the freeway?"

Richard tried to navigate from the parking lot with one hand. "Just about. I'll be there in a half hour."

"A half hour! The reservation was for five minutes ago."

"Maybe we should meet there?" He braced himself as he said this. Silence from her end.

"I'm really sorry, honey," Richard said. "This afternoon was crazy."

He could hear her sigh.

"All right," she said, her voice tight. "I'll meet you there."

"I love you..." he said, but he wasn't sure she heard him.

Richard knew she'd calm down once they were together. What Janet didn't know was that he'd booked them into a great hotel right on the beach. That overtime he was earning would come in handy.

He didn't think they were hurting financially, but they were beginning to depend on his overtime to make their monthly minimum payment obligations. Janet earned six figures, and now Richard's promotion would make things even better.

Richard walked into the restaurant to see Janet sitting alone at a table overlooking the ocean. She looked beautiful in a stunning dress that showed off everything he loved. But he felt like he was walking on eggshells.

"You look amazing," Richard said, testing the waters as he sat down.

Janet was not at all pleased to have been sitting alone for twenty minutes wondering if her husband were going to make it to their one-year wedding anniversary. But she bottled it up rather than spoiling the evening with a fight. "Thank you," she said, "I thought I would surprise you with a new dress."

"I love it," Richard replied. He leaned over for a kiss. "I'm all yours, all weekend."

"Really?" Janet relaxed a little at his caress.

"And," he said proudly, "I've got some great news."

Janet took in a deep breath. "I do, too."

The News

"How far along are you?" Richard asked, trying to conceal his shock after she told him. He looked at her waist as if expecting it to inflate before his eyes.

"I'm not sure. I took the test last week, so it can't be more than a month. What do you think?" Janet asked. Neither of them had planned this. When they'd talked about it, they agreed they wanted to wait a few years before having kids.

"Well, I wasn't expecting this, but we will make it work." Richard knew that wasn't the best answer immediately after he said it, but he didn't have the past week that Janet had to get used to the idea of having a baby. Richard did want kids, but he wasn't prepared for it yet. "You know, we never did add you to my health insurance. Do you know how that will work?" Richard asked, now beginning to think about how much this might cost.

Right on cue, Janet reacted. "Is that the first thing you're thinking about, insurance?"

Now backpedaling, he said, "No, of course not. I just want you and the baby to be covered. I'm sure everything will work out. It's going to be great. I'm happy we're having a family." He took her hand. "And now my news is even better. I got promoted to detective."

Janet's eyes widened. Richard had been wanting this for a long time, but it would mean longer hours and maybe even more dangerous work. "That's fantastic, honey."

"Yeah, maybe we can start thinking about a house."

"Oh, Richard!" Janet then smiled a real smile, for the first time that evening. They started giggling like school kids.

They decided not to stress about money and instead talked about the baby. The more they talked about it, the more excited they both got. Seeing Richard get excited about decorating the baby room put Janet at ease.

By the end of the evening they were having fun bantering back and forth about what names they wanted for their first child. Then Richard sprang his next surprise—their luxurious weekend at the beach.

Uncertainty

Janet couldn't have been happier with the hotel room Richard picked. It overlooked the ocean, where they slept in late on both Saturday and Sunday.

Richard watched Janet sleep that Sunday morning. She lay there, with the ocean breeze blowing over them through the sheer curtains, in the glow of the morning sun, her blonde hair messy on her pillow and her tan smooth skin waiting to be touched—

He smiled as he ordered room service. The smell of bacon and coffee woke her up, and she stretched.

"Great, breakfast! I'm starving," she said.

He grinned and rubbed her belly. "Eating for two, huh?"

She kissed him and took a bite of bacon. "Will you still love me when I'm big as a house?"

"More than ever."

His arms went around her for a bigger kiss, but she pushed around him to keep eating. He laughed and joined her.

Richard was enjoying the weekend, but as they cuddled in bed after breakfast, he started thinking about how things were going to change when the baby came. He was excited, but also a bit afraid. He knew he would be treading on thin ice, but couldn't help asking, "Have you thought about whether you'll work or not after we have the baby?"

"Why do you ask? I hadn't really thought about it," Janet answered, and then paused before finishing. "But I don't want to be one of those absentee parents. My dad was like that. I think I want to stay home at least until he goes off to school."

"He?" Richard asked, surprised. "You know that already?"

"No," Janet grinned. "Not yet. But you want a boy, don't you?"

"Oh, I don't care, either way is fine," Richard answered with a bit of a white lie.

"I didn't mean to get your hopes up." Janet said, still teasing, but also to cover up that she knew he didn't like her answer about leaving work. She was earning well over half of their income, and they didn't have any money saved. They already felt pinched each month as it was, so her quitting her job sounded impossible—even irresponsible.

Richard looked out at the ocean, trying to enjoy the morning. But he couldn't stop thinking about money. "I don't understand how we will make it if you quit your job."

Janet, slightly irritated, replied, "It's going to be fine."

"How?" Richard asked, his voice edged a bit with frustration. "We're barely making it now."

Janet snapped, "I can't stand being worried about money all the time!" She was almost shouting.

Richard didn't understand why she was flaring up. "We have to talk about it sometime, don't we?" He'd forgotten about pregnancy hormones.

Janet climbed out of bed and headed for the bathroom. "All you do is work overtime now and talk about how much we need the money. This is the last I want to hear about it!"

Retail Therapy

A few months passed since their weekend getaway. Although they left the resort that weekend arguing, they both apologized the following morning and hadn't argued since. Janet could sense Richard was still very stressed about money. But she refused to discuss it—it still made her too mad.

Besides, as Janet grew bigger, there were other things to talk about. With prenatal visits, birthing classes, and parenting books, their time was filled with preparing for the new baby. When they broke the news to their parents, the glee reached epic proportions, especially from Janet's mother.

With each passing week, Richard clocked more and more hours while Janet's desire to be at work was dwindling. She was so distracted by her pregnancy that all she wanted to do was stay home and work on the nursery.

Janet's job gave her a lot of flexibility to set her own schedule. She became more efficient and began to work only the first half of the day. Since she was paid a salary plus commissions, as long as she had enough orders to meet her quota, she managed to stay out of trouble and still get her work done early each day. However, her sales volume was decreasing.

It seemed the less Janet worked, the more time Richard spent fighting crime. He hadn't noticed her decreasing paychecks, because she had the job of family bookkeeper. But she was home more often, so she felt his absence even more.

Janet understood why Richard was working so much, but she was lonely. She was also becoming physically uncomfortable as pregnancy progressed, and none of her clothes were right.

One afternoon in May, Janet could not get herself to do any work at all. But she also didn't feel like sitting around the house alone either. There was only one solution—retail therapy.

She called her friend from high school, Stephanie. They'd been giggling at clothing stores together since the ninth grade. They both came from families with large credit lines. Stephanie was glad to meet her for lunch at Santa Barbara's Paseo Nuevo mall.

"I've got a new credit card I'm dying to break in," Stephanie said as she plopped her purse in the seat at the table. "How about we try that new boutique on the main level?"

"Okay," Janet agreed, "but I also need to stop at the maternity store." She was determined not to be like so many other pregnant moms she had seen, wearing their husbands' sweatpants and oversized T-shirts.

The two shopped all afternoon and even got their nails done. Stephanie's husband David worked in finance, and Stephanie talked and talked about the house they were about to buy.

"It's gorgeous," Stephanie said. "Marble tile in the master bath and a Jacuzzi out back—we love it. We're closing next week."

Janet tried not to be jealous—she didn't know when she and Richard would be able to get a house. But after returning to the car with several bags of new clothes and freshly manicured nails, she felt great. Pampering herself was just the therapy she needed.

When she got home, Janet was surprised that Richard's car was already in the garage. She must have been shopping longer than she thought. She left the bags in the trunk.

Hunting Trip

When Janet walked in, Richard was on his cell and greeted her with a kiss. He was talking to his friend Jake about their annual trip coming up in September. Every year, Richard, Jake, and a couple of their friends would leave for a week or two on a big hunting trip.

Janet frowned when she realized who was on the phone. That year, the baby was due right when they'd be going.

Richard signed off and put his arms around Janet's growing belly as she pulled out the take-out menu for some Chinese food.

"So," Janet said, not wanting to sound upset, "planning the trip?"

Richard hugged her closer. "The good news is, the guys want to go earlier this year. So it won't conflict with the baby."

Janet was surprised. "I thought hunting season didn't start until September."

"There's actually no set season where we're thinking of going."

Richard sounded a little hesitant, so Janet turned around to look at him. "And where would that be?"

He looked at a spot over her head on the wall and braced himself. "Uh, Africa."

"Africa?!" Janet exclaimed, raising her voice more out of surprise than anything else. "Why Africa?"

"Jake thought it would be something different, and it sounds exciting," Richard answered. "I don't think they have any rules over there, so we can go whenever we want. The guys are saying they could go in August."

"Isn't that kind of far? How much is that going to cost?" Janet asked, but then she blushed, remembering the piles of bags she had in the car trunk. However, she was also a bit shocked by the idea of him leaving the country, and so close to the baby's arrival.

Richard had no idea how much it was going to cost, but had already realized it was going to be way more than his past trips. "We always get that tax refund every year," he said. "We could put the trip on the credit cards and then pay it off when the money comes."

"That's months away," Janet objected. "And we have no idea if we'll even get a refund."

"Why wouldn't we? Don't we always?" Richard was worried because as soon as Jake suggested the trip, Richard had already begun mentally spending that refund.

"Don't you remember? The tax guy warned us that because we were beginning to make so much money we needed to change our deductions or we would probably have to pay this year," Janet said.

Richard hadn't yet taken the time to figure out the taxes for that year. He'd never felt comfortable with the entire process, and had even neglected to file one year before they were married. But Janet had dealt with the tax stuff the prior year, and this year was his turn. "Did we change the deductions?" he asked.

"No, because he wanted to charge us two or three hundred bucks to help us with tax planning and it didn't seem worth it," Janet said.

"Two or three hundred—what the heck for?" Richard asked.

"I don't know. It was about tax savings and adjusting our deductions or something like that. I didn't understand it and didn't want to spend the money, but he warned me we were probably going to have to pay taxes this year," Janet said.

Richard was getting frustrated. "You should have done it if we are going to have to pay," he said, but he really had no idea if she should have spent the money on the tax planning. He just wanted to go to Africa.

Janet slammed the take-out menu on the counter. "Well, maybe if you were on top of things this year I wouldn't have to make all these decisions by myself," she snapped back. "I'm sick of having to figure everything out." She stormed out of the kitchen.

Baby Buying

With only about a month until the baby was due, Richard found himself doing a different kind of hunting than he'd planned. At Janet's insistence, he'd given up the idea of the trip with the guys for that year. They couldn't figure out how to pay for it, and babies were sometimes known to come early. Janet couldn't see having him leave the country when she was eight months pregnant.

He knew she was right, but it didn't help that while Jake and the guys were hunting big game in South Africa, Richard and Janet were spending every weekend hunting for baby furniture, car seats, and everything else they would need.

That weekend, Janet's parents, Marge and Phil, came along with them to shop. Richard was beyond tired of their weekly trips to find the perfect crib. Phil was about as bored as Richard, but Marge joined with Janet to coo over baby things.

"Look at this cute comforter!" Marge said at the local big box baby store.

Janet nodded, focused on the cribs. "Do you like this one?" she asked Richard, pointing to the third one she'd shown him since they got there.

Richard, jolted from his reverie, answered, "That one's great."

"Never had all these choices when we had Janet," Phil said. He clapped Richard on the back. "What you really need to be thinking about is a house."

Richard nodded with tight lips. He always felt at a disadvantage around Phil, who was a self-made millionaire of sorts. His car dealership had generated enough for him to raise Janet in a lavish style. And Marge always wanted her little girl to have the finest of everything.

"Oh, I love all these little shoes," Marge said. "Doesn't it take you back, honey?"

"Sure," Phil said. "To every scraped knee, orthodontics bill, college tuition—"

Richard's eyes widened.

"Oh, stop," Marge said, swatting at Phil. "You're making Richard nervous."

"I think I like this one," Janet said to her husband.

Richard stepped over to check the price tag. Sure enough, it was more expensive than the other two. "Isn't this the same as the one at the door?"

"The one that was on sale?" Janet said. "Now don't get cheap! Don't we want the best?"

Richard wanted to say he didn't see what difference it would make, but he held his tongue. "Sure, we want the best."

"We'll help, of course," Marge offered, "if it's too much of a stretch."

Richard gritted his teeth and avoided looking at his father-in-law. "No, it's not a stretch. We're fine."

Janet was about to get angry at Richard's attitude, but then she remembered how disappointed he had been about giving up the hunting trip. She tucked her arm into his. "Are you just saying that or do you mean it?"

"No, I'm serious. This one will look nice in the nursery and the white will go with everything else," Richard said, trying to sound interested.

She reached up to give him a kiss, right in front of her parents. "Thanks, honey. Let's get this one."

"No more looking at cribs?" Richard said hopefully.

Janet laughed. "Nope! We're done!"

Marge chimed in, "But we'll get you these blankets. And bibs. And shoes."

Phil groaned as everyone laughed. But Richard's eyes swept around the store of baby paraphernalia like it was a jungle, and he was surrounded by lions.

Everything Changes

A few days later, Janet's contractions started as she and Richard browsed another store to find baby items. Richard broke all driving records getting home to pick up all of her stuff, but Janet then insisted on touching up her make-up and hair before leaving for the hospital.

Richard thought it was crazy to be fussing over make-up, but Janet knew it might be a while before she got another chance. Richard was in a mild panic, assuming there would soon be a roadside delivery like on television if they didn't hurry up.

Once they got to the hospital and the nurses took over, Richard was a bit more at peace. Everything went smoothly, more or less, and Janet was a real trooper. Soon Richard, in a daze, was cutting the umbilical cord for a healthy, squalling baby boy.

As Richard lay beside a dozing Janet on the tiny hospital bed and they cuddled their now quiet baby, his heart filled with an entirely new feeling. He suddenly knew he would do anything for that little squirming bundle. He'd had no idea that fatherhood would hit him so hard.

Once Janet was sound asleep, Richard went home, still in a state of euphoria. Nothing at home looked good enough anymore. They had to get a bigger place. He was glad now they'd gotten the top-of-the-line car seat, even though it took him almost an hour to figure out how to secure it in the back of the car.

The next day, Richard walked out of the hospital proudly holding his son, Matthew. Janet was still exhausted from the delivery so she was happy to be wheeled to the car by a nurse.

Richard had never driven so cautiously in his life. Now that his newborn was in the back seat, each turn was as careful as taking his driver's test when he was sixteen. He never wished he was back to working in a patrol car as much as that moment, so he could write tickets to the idiots driving so quickly past him.

Once at home, with Janet and baby tucked safely into bed, Richard went online. This was his first moment to think, and his head was filled with one thing—money. Time to look at some houses. Time to think about life insurance. Time to figure things out.

House Hunting

The first week after Matthew was born was both exciting and exhausting. Richard took the time off to help get Matthew into a routine. Janet was in a haze that week because she had not recovered from giving birth and was up every three hours feeding the baby.

Richard tried to get up with Janet every few hours, but quickly got frustrated because he wasn't able to help. Janet appreciated it at first, but was soon too tired to even notice. Eventually they agreed there was little point in him waking up with her.

Instead, Richard spent a lot of time at the computer while the other two napped. He found a nifty mortgage calculator that showed him how easy it would be to afford a house. In fact, it seemed like they could buy twice the house they had now, for less than they were paying in rent. He didn't understand some of the fine print, like "adjustable rate" or "PMI" or "low, low percent down." But the calculator made him wonder why they'd waited at all.

Then he started checking listings online. There were great neighborhoods with houses in what the calculator said was their price range. He decided that as soon as Janet was feeling stronger, they'd start looking.

Eventually the new family settled into a routine. Richard was busy at work and happy to come home to see his new baby. Janet was still taking time off, receiving state disability payments. These were nowhere near what they had been earning previously, but Richard was working a lot of overtime trying to make up the difference.

Janet had joined Richard at the computer one night between feedings and had seen some of the listings the mortgage calculator said they could afford. The pictures included kitchens with marble counters, huge two-car garages, and shining master bathrooms—just like Stephanie's house. Janet got excited at the idea of raising their baby in such nice surroundings.

The weekend before Thanksgiving, when Matthew was three months old, they decided to leave him with Marge and Phil and do a tour of some open houses. One house in particular kept their interest with its lovely eat-in kitchen and fenced in backyard.

The real estate agent showing the house saw their interest and got a gleam in her eye. She whipped out her calculator. "With a low down payment, your monthly payment would be this."

"That's really low," Richard said in surprise.

"This is a buyer's market," the agent assured them. "Great bargains are being snapped up."

Janet said, "I've heard of not having to put down any money."

The agent hesitated. "That's not so common anymore," she said. "Putting down just 3–5% is easy, though."

Janet and Richard left with the agent's card and a purchase-and-sale agreement form.

Thanksgiving of Money

In a moment of new-parent insanity, Janet had told the family she wanted to have Thanksgiving at their house that year. She was feeling fully domesticated and wanted to show off, but didn't realize how much work it would be. Richard took care of borrowing some small tables and chairs from their neighbors who would be out of town, but it was Janet wrestling with the turkey in the kitchen since dawn.

Richard's father and sister, Mike and Michelle, got there early with a bouquet of flowers and some wine. Janet put Michelle to work arranging the flowers in a vase, while Richard and Mike set the table. Little Matthew slept through all the commotion in his swinging chair.

Michelle gabbed as she cut the stems. "You know I started an online business," she said. "Making those bags you liked?"

"Oh, yeah," Janet said, distracted. "The ones with the hot glue designs?"

"Yep. I think they could really sell. I just need a little seed money." Michelle looked at Janet sidelong, but Janet was too focused on the mashed potatoes to notice. "I didn't know if you guys wanted to back me at all."

Janet turned to her in surprise. Her immediate thoughts were,

With what? They'd always kept their money issues hidden from their families, trying to show a prosperous front. Now Janet thought that maybe they looked too prosperous. "I don't know, Michelle, I'd have to talk with Richard."

"I'd only need a couple thousand."

"For what?" Richard said, coming into the kitchen for the glasses.

"The business I'm starting."

"What happened to that thing last year, the special food for pets?" he asked her.

"Oh, that had too much overhead," Michelle said, as though she knew all about business. "But this would be just me, making the bags and selling them, in one of those online shops. I'd give you ten percent owner-ship." Her tone took on a bit of a wheedle.

"What about Dad?"

"Oh, he never has any money, you know that. And Mom's new husband already said no."

Richard's mom had remarried a guy with some cash, who was apparently too smart to be pressured into Michelle's ideas. Richard exchanged glances with Janet. They both knew they didn't have the money, even if this business were a good idea. "We'll think about it, sis."

That was just the beginning of the Thanksgiving of Money.

When Phil and Marge arrived, Marge noticed immediately that Janet was frazzled, and she got cracking in the kitchen. Soon things were set and Janet could relax a little.

Phil, avoiding the kitchen and any chores, zeroed in on all the listing sheets sitting on the desk near the kitchen. "I see you've been looking at houses," he said as they all sat down to eat.

"We saw so many nice places," Janet said. Each house had looked beautiful, but had one or two things wrong with them—too near a busy street, or poor new construction, or not enough windows. "The one with three bedrooms was nice, but so dark. And one with the huge kitchen would need a total remodel."

Mike, Richard's father, had also been a long-time police officer. "What do you need three bedrooms for?" he asked, gruff. "You're just starting out."

Janet glanced down the table at Richard, who was focused on gaining a new skill set—slicing the turkey. "We're thinking we should get the best one we can afford," she said, "so Matthew will be in a nice neighborhood."

Janet's father Phil reached over for the listing sheets. "What are the asking prices?" When he saw the numbers, he nearly spat out his drink. "These numbers are huge! What kind of mortgage would you have?"

That got Richard's attention. "The calculators online said we could afford them."

"And the real estate agent was so friendly," Janet added.

Phil snorted. "Did they include PMI or taxes?"

Richard had no idea. He and Janet both shrugged.

"Look, kids, that will raise your monthly payment by hundreds of dollars. And I assume you were only looking at fixed rates."

Janet bit her lip. "There was something that said 'adjustable.'"

"No way," Phil said. "You can't get an adjustable loan. That will kill you later. Look, if you don't know what you're doing with this stuff, better to stay put."

Richard flushed. His father-in-law always knew how to rub him the wrong way.

"Renting was always good enough for us," Richard's dad Mike threw in for good measure. "No need to saddle yourself with the huge responsibility of a house."

"What the guys mean," Marge said to soften the blow, "is that you're fine where you are now. Why rush? And take the time to figure out the ins and outs of home ownership. There's a lot to learn. We learned a lot of it the hard way. Remember, honey?"

Phil grunted, not wanting to admit he'd not always known everything. But it made Richard feel better to have Marge point it out.

"You're right," Richard said. "There's no rush."

A loud knock at the door made everyone jump. Janet rose to answer it.

"Uncle Roger!" Janet said in surprise as she hugged the new arrival.

"Yes, your favorite uncle's here. Can't keep me away from free food." Uncle Roger was Phil's brother and ran some sort of insurance business. He chucked Matthew under the chin and sat right next to Richard. "New baby, huh?" he said. "You gotta start thinking about the future."

The table broke into several conversations, all revolving around money. Michelle cornered Marge to talk about the bag business and to get her thoughts on "raising capital." Richard's dad raised a glass to congratulate his newly married ex-wife *in absentia*—and his own new freedom from paying alimony. Phil continued to lecture Janet about how to buy a house.

But Richard was stuck listening to Roger pitch his life insurance "investment" business. He mostly tuned it out, until Roger said, "What would your wife and child do if something happened to you? How would they eat?" When Roger saw the look on Richard's face, he knew he'd hit a nerve. He reached into his back pocket and pulled out a business card. "Call me," he said.

Christmas

Police work stepped up for the month of December, with so many people on the road partying and shopping. Richard's entire department worked long hours, so he wasn't around to notice how Janet was spending her time.

She'd gotten it down to a science: Get Matthew in the car right before naptime. Drive to mall. Grab some lunch at the food court, then stroll around for a couple hours. The three-month-old slept right through almost everything, and that top-of-the-line stroller had a lot of great places to hang bags.

Richard didn't see the damage until Christmas Eve. When he got back from his annual one day of shopping for presents, he found Janet sitting on the floor in the living room in front of the tree, surrounded by boxes and wrapping paper. Matthew sat in his bouncy chair, chewing on ribbon, while a DVD of *The Grinch* played on TV.

"What is all this stuff?" Richard asked in amazement.

"Santa came early!" Janet said, excited. "This is just like the Christmases when I was growing up." The next morning, her parents were coming over, and she wanted the festivities to be up to snuff.

Richard picked up some baby clothes. "Won't he outgrow these in about ten minutes?" He'd already been astonished at how little wear all those infant clothes got—the ones they only bought five months before.

"But they're so cute. We can donate them later." Janet tied a bow on a package as Richard sifted through the other things.

I'm buying things we're just going to give away? Richard thought. But he said, "These are way too old for him." He held up a puzzle and a book.

"So he can enjoy chewing on them now!" Janet wanted to hang onto her good mood despite Richard's comments. She'd always loved Christmas.

Richard frowned. "It just seems like a bit much for a kid who's primary interest at the moment is what he can get in his mouth. I thought we were saving for a house." Of course, they hadn't yet saved anything; Richard was just bringing this up as ammunition.

On the TV, Cindy Lou Who was just then getting her cup of water. "Oh, stop being a Grinch," Janet said. "This is our first Christmas with our baby."

"I know—"

"Honey, please! You're always telling me what to do. I've always wanted this kind of Christmas for my children. Matthew is more important than anything. We have to give him the best."

Janet wasn't looking at Richard, but he could see the tight stress lines around her lips. He took a deep breath. "We'll talk about saving after the new year?"

"Fine." She slapped some tape on a package, her mood spoiled.

The New Year

For the first time that year, Janet and Richard didn't go out and party on New Year's Eve. Having an infant wiped them out. They were asleep by 9:30 p.m. (right after watching the ball fall in New York City) and up at dawn the next day with Matthew's "Happy New Year" crying.

As the new year started, Janet had something else on her mind. Each day that passed, the more depressed she became just thinking about it.

Janet did not want to go back to work. She managed to hide her feelings from Richard until the very morning she was due back in late January. She woke up sometime around 4:00 a.m. to feed Matthew. After feeding him, she broke down crying.

Richard slowly woke up, groggy, until he realized Janet was crying. He jumped out of bed panicked, fearing something terrible had happened to Matthew.

"What's wrong?" Richard said.

"I just... I just..." Janet tried to explain, but it was hard to get the words out. "I don't want to go back to work!" she finally blurted.

Long before Matthew arrived, they had planned that after about four months she would return to work and Matthew would spend part of the time with Janet's mother while Richard and Janet staggered their schedules to be able to take care of him.

The problem was, now that it was actually happening, Janet couldn't imagine leaving her baby. The day before, Janet had cried almost the entire day. Richard didn't know because he was at work, and when he returned she did her best not to show it.

Janet hadn't wanted to tell Richard how upset she was. She thought Richard would criticize her because he was working and she was upset about having to go to work. Janet felt conflicted. She did not want to leave her baby, but felt it was her responsibility to return to work to help provide for their family. They were already struggling financially before she got pregnant, and now things were even worse.

Richard was shocked. His thoughts jumbled at Janet's exclamation. How would they survive without her six-figure income? But he bit his lip and put his arms around her.

"It's okay, honey. We'll figure something out," he said, not really believing it. "Are you saying you don't want to go back to work *today*?"

Her breath came out in a shudder. "No, I know I have to go back today. I just hate the idea of working forever. I want to be with Matthew."

Relieved, Richard hugged her closer and stroked the fine hairs on Matthew's head. "Let's see how it goes. Maybe in a few months, we won't need so much money."

They looked at each other, both knowing this would never be the case.

New Routine

Janet slowly eased back into working about six hours a day. She would leave the house first in the morning. Richard took care of Matthew until Marge arrived. Then Richard would leave for work, and a few hours later Janet would return and relieve her mother.

It was working out, but Janet did not like it. When she was gone, she missed being home to take care of Matthew and felt like she was losing irreplaceable time during his young years. When she was home, she was lonely. Richard's hours often stretched late into the evening, sometimes even keeping him away until late at night.

The couple rarely spent time together like they had before the baby. They used to go out on dates almost every other night, mostly because neither of them cooked. Now Janet's cooking skills were improving, but there was no one to cook for.

February came and went, their anniversary slipping by with hardly any acknowledgement. Their financial problems had gotten worse, but since they seldom talked, they managed to ignore them. While Janet was on maternity leave, it had become normal for them to use their credit cards to make up the monthly shortage. Now that she was back to work, they continued that habit.

At least since they were going out so little, they charged less to their credit cards each month. But because the balances had gotten so high, they still struggled to make the monthly minimum payments and thus had less money left over. Previously they were trying to pay down the balances each month, and now they were just trying to make the minimum payments.

Despite all this, Richard felt he had a great life. As the Southern California spring progressed, he found he loved his work. He was working so hard and putting in so many hours that it was obvious to those around him that he wouldn't stay a detective forever. When the promotion came to supervisor of their unit in May, he couldn't wait to tell Janet.

"Hi, honey!" Richard's happiness spilled over the phone. "Let's plan something special tonight—I've got some good news."

He'd caught Janet as she was driving over to Stephanie's with Matthew for a quick visit after her rounds with her clients. Janet was glad he had something to be happy about. "Why don't I ask Mom to take Matthew for the night, after I'm done at Stephanie's?" she said.

Richard didn't realize how much he missed spending time alone with Janet until that exact moment. "Oh, that sounds fabulous. Just you and me, alone for an evening. I'd love that."

Janet smiled. "Okay, let me put together a nice dinner. See you around seven?"

"I can't wait." Richard hung up, a huge grin on his face.

Keeping Up

Janet pulled into Stephanie's circular cobblestoned driveway, which wound around a new little fountain, and parked by the front door. As she was taking seven-month-old Matthew out of his car seat, Stephanie came out.

"Let me help you!" Stephanie said. She cooed and grabbed Matthew, who grinned and drooled on her, while Janet hefted the diaper bag to her shoulder and looked around.

"Gosh, Steph, your yard looks great."

"Oh, we just had that fountain put in. Increases the curb appeal," Stephanie said. "Come inside!"

Soon they were in Stephanie's family room, with their big screen TV and modern furniture. Janet plopped on the floor with Matthew and sat him up on his play mat. He instantly dove to chew on the squeaky attachments.

"So cute," Stephanie said, not a maternal bone in her body. She pointed out the French doors to the back. "Did you see the new flowers around the Jacuzzi?"

"Very nice." Janet fought her usual jealousy at Stephanie's gorgeous place. She didn't know when she and Richard would ever be able to afford a place like this. But Stephanie had married money, and now had all this to show for it.

"How are things with you and Richard?" Stephanie asked.

"Oh, okay. We don't see each other enough, but he said he'd be home tonight to celebrate something about work."

"Work, work, work. All these men do is work. You've got to get him to live a little."

"The thing is, I think he loves his job. I just feel like I get stuck—" Janet stopped. She didn't want to air her dirty laundry to Stephanie. But she had no one to talk to lately.

"Stuck how?" Stephanie sounded genuinely sympathetic.

"It's nothing really, and I know we're just adjusting to having a baby. But I feel like I'm doing it all. Matthew, and the house, and the bills, and the cooking...it's all on me. Richard's never there. It's like he feels that since he's providing, he doesn't have to be part of it." She ignored, or forgot, that Richard took care of Matthew every morning, usually did all the laundry, and handled all the yard work.

Stephanie frowned. "But you're still working, right?"

"I'm not working as much as before, but yeah, I still bring in almost half of our income." Janet suddenly felt resentful, like this was crystallizing everything she had been feeling.

Stephanie shook her head. "That's not fair for you to be doing all that. And you don't even like your job."

Janet's lips tightened. Stephanie was right. *How did this happen?* Janet thought. *How did I wind up doing everything?*

Stephanie watched her face. "Look, I know this isn't in your mind yet, but I've heard of a good family/divorce lawyer."

Janet turned to her in shock. "What? I don't want a divorce!" But even as she said that, she knew things couldn't go on as they had been. She just didn't know how to talk to Richard about it.

"Let me send you her information. So you have it, if you need it." Stephanie went to the computer in the room—it seemed like every room had a computer—and clicked around. "There, I emailed it to you. Just in case."

When Janet left Stephanie's, it only took a quick phone call to convince Grandma to take her "little man" for the night. Janet dropped Matthew off at Marge's, feeling a twinge of guilt. She yearned to spend more time being a mom, and here she was sending her baby off again. But a night with Richard would be important. They really needed to reconnect—she felt this as strongly as he had.

Meth Gets in the Way

The afternoon had been speeding by for Richard, with congratulations all around from the squad about his promotion. But then, the call came in. It was his informant for his prize case, with late breaking news.

For months, Richard had been cultivating this informant's trust in the pursuit of one of the largest methamphetamine dealers in Ventura, who was smuggling the drugs in from Mexico. The narcotic unit had been chasing this drug dealer for several years, but it was only because of Richard's informant that they had a hope of catching him.

"The truck just crossed the border," the informant whispered from whatever pre-paid cell phone he was using.

Richard could picture him there on the street, glancing over his shoulders nervously. The man was putting his life on the line.

"Got it," Richard said. "When will it be there?"

"At the address I told you. Three hours."

The line went dead.

When Richard hung up the phone, he paused for a second. Here was this huge meth deal going down, one that would bag a major drug dealer and take a lot of drugs off the street, and all he could think about was how angry Janet would be. He checked the clock. It was only two-thirty. If the truck arrived as promised, he could be done by six, or six-thirty tops. He decided not to call Janet—yet—and instead set his mind to co-ordinating the team for the bust.

Richard's plan was for the detectives to follow the dealer into his house. Once the truck arrived, they would call the SWAT team to make the arrest. The drug dealer was known to have many guns in the house, so the SWAT team had already been put on standby and was preparing for the arrest.

*   *   *

Janet took a nap—which felt really good—and began to plan dinner. Her cooking skills had improved in the prior months, so she thought she'd try a mushroom risotto with chicken. After a quick trip to the grocery store, she set to work, humming as she chopped and diced in the kitchen.

*   *   *

Traffic. No schedule in L.A. is safe with all the traffic. Over two hours went by, but the drug dealer hadn't yet left to meet the truck. Richard and his team figured he was getting ongoing reports as to the truck's progress up the coast, and wouldn't start out until the truck was nearby. The men stationed surreptitiously at the address said they saw no activity.

Richard bit his lip. Five o'clock. Time to call Janet.

* * *

"That meth will just have to wait at his house until tomorrow!" Janet said, her voice heading up a decibel.

Richard winced. "But it's a huge case out of Mexico. The truck is on its way. We have to get him tonight."

She said nothing.

"Look," he said, "I'll call you as soon as I can. I love you."

He heard the bleep as her phone disconnected. He shook his head, just as the phone buzzed again.

"He's on the move," one of his men told him.

Hallelujah, Richard thought as he headed for the car. *Maybe this will be quick.*

Confrontation

At seven o'clock, Janet stood in the kitchen, glaring at the risotto. If they didn't eat it soon, it would turn into inedible goo.

She was just out of the shower in her bathrobe. She'd wanted to look nice for Richard when he got home, but now all the energy deflated out of her. He hadn't answered her calls for the last forty-five minutes, so he was probably in the middle of arresting God knows who. He wouldn't show up for dinner—he would have called if he were on the way. So, instead she threw on some sweats and dished herself up a heaping plate.

Without Matthew there, the house was empty and lonely. She went over to the desk, where bills piled high and the computer blinked. Maybe at least she could get some of that figured out now that she had a spare moment. But every time she got the checkbook out and went online to check their account balances, it made her angry. She was coming up short and wasn't finding any answers.

Hours went by. Janet hated going to bed alone, and often stayed up hoping Richard would come home soon. When she finally heard the car drive up, she was in a fine state.

He walked in, tired. "Hey," he said.

"Where have you been?" Janet tried not to, but she did snap a bit.

"Well, we caught the guy and the courier. Shots were fired."

Janet's face dropped. "Are you all right?" she asked, visions of him being shot on duty running through her mind.

"I'm fine. No one got hurt, but there was tons of paperwork."

"Oh, right. Paperwork." She tried not to sound sarcastic, but he could have called. "Do you want some dinner?"

"I'm starving." Richard followed her into the kitchen. "What have you been doing all night, without Matthew?"

"Paying bills," Janet answered. "Trying to figure it out."

His smile was wan. "Well, I have some good news then," he said. "I just got promoted to supervisor."

Janet froze, serving spoon hovering over the pot. "What?"

"Yeah, that should bring in more money. Maybe that will help."

"But you'll be gone even more now!" Janet, exhausted, couldn't help it. It was all getting to be too much.

"I thought you wanted me to earn more," Richard said defensively.

"I'm sick of you always being gone. You're never here anymore. When do you plan to be part of this family?" Janet said.

"What do you want from me? Do you want me to bring in more money, or be home more?" Richard asked, frustrated. He wished he hadn't even come home. "I can go back you know, there's still plenty to do with all the bookings. The guys are still there."

"And when you are here, I'm gone!" At that very moment, it clicked for Janet. She missed the fun they used to have together and the time and attention Richard gave her. Now she rarely got attention and he was always working. "I'm the one who should be leaving! I'm stuck here all the time, and you're out—getting shot at—"

The next thing Richard knew, Janet was crying. He rubbed his eyes. What the hell were they going to do?

The Lawyer

Janet and Richard gave each other a lot of space the next morning. She left without saying goodbye.

But once in the car, she sat there for a while, thinking. Impulsively, she reached for her phone and scrolled through emails looking for the number Stephanie had sent her. *It can't hurt to get some information*, she thought. She left a message asking for an appointment, and she heard later that morning that the lawyer was available the next day.

Once at the appointment, the attorney had a lot of questions about Janet's situation. She handled both divorce and family cases, so her primary concern was what would be best for Matthew. Janet was glad the lawyer had this point of view—it reassured her she wouldn't harm Matthew, no matter what happened with Richard. And, it was a relief to finally have someone to talk to about everything. Janet found herself downloading a lot of her thoughts and feelings. But the lawyer kept circling back around to money.

"So it sounds like you have some consumer debt, an unclear picture of your tax status, and not much retirement as of yet." The lawyer had been taking notes the whole time.

Janet admitted it, even though she felt foolish. "That's what most of our fights are about—money."

The lawyer leaned back in her chair. She had a kind look on her face, but it was shrewd, like she knew more about Janet's marriage than Janet did herself. "I never like to kick off a divorce when the financial situation is tenuous," she said. "It makes things very hard in the long run, especially for the woman, and consequently, the children. It's much better to have the finances on solid footing first."

"Really?" Janet asked in surprise.

"Really." The lawyer flipped open a plastic folder of business cards and handed one to Janet across the desk. "I suggest you consult with this financial advisor I know."

Janet took the card. "Danny Venegas."

"I highly recommend him—he's a Fee-Only advisor."

Janet looked at her blankly.

The lawyer explained. "The traditional and most common way advisors are paid is through commissions. Commissions are typically paid when an investment or insurance product is either bought or sold. If you aren't paying fees directly to your insurance or investment advisor, you most likely are working with a commissioned advisor who receives a percentage of each transaction."

"That sounds like my uncle Roger," Janet said, remembering his talking with Richard at Thanksgiving. "He sells insurance investments."

"Right," the lawyer said. "Fee-Only is different. The Fee-Only model can be a flat annual retainer, by the hour, or an annual fee based on a percentage of your investment assets. Fee-Only advisors do not receive any commissions or kickbacks from the products they recommend. They also tend to be more comprehensive and objective, because they are paid the same regardless of which investments you choose. They'll look at your entire financial package, including budgeting or tax issues, rather than just stock or insurance. Does that make sense?"

"It does, actually." Janet shook the cobwebs from the part of her brain that dealt with money. It was time to figure it out, if only for Matthew's sake.

"Don't get tricked by advisors who are fee-based. They sound like they are Fee-Only, but they do get commissions for products they sell and they charge additional fees for advice. It may appear less expensive, but their advice can be biased by commissions they earn that will add up." The lawyer nodded to the business card. "Again, Danny is definitely a Fee-Only advisor and will have your best interests at heart."

"Is he expensive?"

"Not compared to how much he'll be helping you. Why don't you consult with him first, and then get back to me if you want to move forward with divorce proceedings?"

Just hearing the word "divorce" made Janet wince. "Okay." She left that appointment with a lot to think about. Surprisingly, she felt better than she had in months.

Insurance Pressure

Richard, too, was taking action. While he knew he had been doing his best, Janet had a point. Maybe he wasn't paying enough attention to the details of family life.

He got to thinking. She'd seemed pretty upset that he might get hurt on the job. He remembered what Uncle Roger had said at Thanksgiving. True, this was the uncle that Marge tried to keep from the liquor, but he'd had some interesting things to say about insurance to anyone who would listen. Roger's one comment still stuck in Richard's mind. "What would your wife and child do if something happened to you? How would they eat?"

So, about a week later, Richard found himself in Roger's office.

Thank goodness he's not asking too many questions, Richard thought. Once he'd called, Roger had set up an appointment immediately. Richard was already intimated being in the office and didn't think he would have the right answers anyway.

"Good to see you, Richard! You're doing the right thing for your family," Roger said, full of bluster.

"Yes, Janet and I think we need some security now that little Matthew is here," Richard answered, although of course he hadn't discussed it with her yet.

"You've come to the right place," Roger said. "I represent a company called Trans-International. We have an investment product that will be perfect for you. The money you invest into it will grow tax-free and set you up for retirement. And it will protect you and Janet in case one of you passes away; you'll get a tax-free life insurance benefit."

"'Tax-free' sounds pretty good. I think that's one of our problems. We are paying too much in taxes." Richard tried to sound like he understood their financial situation.

Roger asked some formality questions such as their ages, address and such, and then was already filling out some paperwork. Richard was surprised at how fast and easy this all seemed. Actually, it was a little too fast.

"How much does this cost?" Richard asked. He wasn't even sure if asking the fee was the right question. He felt like he did when he'd bought his motorcycle—the salesman just forged right ahead.

"You don't have to pay me anything," Roger answered. "You can either write a check for your monthly investment or have it automatically deducted from your checking account each month. That's better so you don't forget it."

"Uh, I need to talk it over with Janet first," Richard said to stall. "She manages the money month-to-month."

"Let's get your account started today, and then we can have her come in later to discuss her own account," Roger pressured.

Richard started getting uncomfortable. It was being hurried way too much, but he did want to go home to Janet and impress her that he'd done something to help the family. "What happens if I sign up for this and later change my mind?" Richard asked.

"You need to think long term with these types of investments," Roger answered. "You're better off making a commitment for several years, wouldn't you agree?"

He'd answered by asking his own question. "Yeah, I suppose," Richard said. "But I still have to talk to Janet."

"She's got a lot on her mind right now, with the baby and all. How about you take care of it for her?" Roger said. He held out the pen for Richard to sign.

Near Miss

*B*ack at home that afternoon—early for once—Richard fell into the couch and began reading through the life insurance brochure Roger had given him until Janet woke up from her nap. Matthew was sleeping, too, and the house was nice and quiet.

The uncle had given Richard a big colorful brochure with a bunch of charts and graphs that didn't make any sense. It also had a bunch of stock photographs with politically correct, ethnically mixed people, smiling in parks and running on beaches holding hands, which seemed almost humorous.

It was convincing, but the program seemed so expensive. For each monthly payment, or "investment," as the brochure called it, they could probably get a new car.

Janet came out of the bedroom, a little groggy.

"Hi, honey," she said in her sweet sleepy voice. Richard loved her like this. She cuddled up beside him on the couch.

"I have a surprise for you." Richard said.

Janet perked up. "Really, what is it?"

"I was meeting with your uncle. You know, the insurance investment guy."

"Roger?" Janet's voice became a little alarmed. She remembered what her lawyer said about Fee-Only. "What did you see him for?"

"You were right, I need to get more involved. I thought we should get some form of security now that Matthew is here," Richard explained. "I went to talk with Roger to try to get some help. He recommended we invest in some kind of tax-free insurance investment thing."

But Janet knew her uncle. "What kind of 'investment' is it?"

"I didn't understand it, but it's supposed to save us on taxes, and besides, we need to start planning for retirement since we haven't done much of anything yet." Richard realized how little he knew about it the moment he tried to explain it to Janet.

"You don't understand it and you signed us up for it?" Janet asked, a bit of panic in her voice.

"No, no, I didn't sign us up. He pressured me to, but I told him I needed to talk with you first. He gave me this paperwork so we can look it over." Richard handed her the brochure. "Don't worry. I wouldn't get us locked into something without talking with you first."

"Well, thank you for looking into it," Janet said, relieved that Richard did not get them into any contracts. "Let's talk about this later." She was skeptical of her uncle. It wasn't that she didn't trust him, because he was family, but he was a good salesman. She wasn't completely sure he would put their interests above his own. She got up and stretched. "What do you want for dinner?"

"How about the frozen enchiladas?"

"Good, that's easy," Janet said on her way to the kitchen. "Would you get the mail?"

"Sure." But Richard wasn't ready for what he would find there.

The Fight

Stunned and confused, Richard came back into the house from the mailbox with an open letter in his hand. The return address looked legal, so he'd opened it without looking at the addressee. Now it turned out to be from some divorce/family lawyer following up with Janet on an appointment she'd had.

"What is this?!" Richard said once he was in the kitchen.

Janet turned to him in surprise. Her heart dropped as she took the letter he thrust at her and read it. The attorney was asking about next steps and had sent a bill for the consult.

"Oh, honey—" Janet started to explain, but Richard was too upset to let her.

"You're thinking about divorce? What's the matter with you?" He was yelling like he never had before.

Janet backed away. "I was just getting some information—"

"Fabulous." Richard's voice dripped with sarcasm. "I'm out there, busting my ass, and you're secretly meeting with lawyers to figure out how to fleece me." This was Richard's nightmare—his dad had always said divorce was a financial disaster and that Richard's mother had taken him for everything he had.

Now Janet got mad, too. "I was doing no such thing. I was trying to see how to do the best thing for Matthew."

"The best thing for Matthew? As if you care about him." Richard's hurt made him irrational. "You just want everything your own way all the time."

This was a slap to Janet. "How can you say that? I went back to work—"

"Barely. And your spending all the time is why we're in this mess to begin with."

"What?!" she shouted. "What about that motorcycle in the garage and the big screen TV and the trips to Africa?"

"I didn't go to Africa!" Richard was so mad now he could hardly see straight. He knew if they went on too much longer things would get out of hand. He grabbed the letter from her and threw it on the floor. "Fine. Get a divorce. See if I care." He stormed out to take a long ride on the bike and try to cool down.

Janet felt sick about it as she heard his motorcycle roar off. *I hope he's careful.* But then she thought about some of the things he'd said—like everything was her fault—and her blood started to boil again. *Maybe this divorce is the best idea I've had in a long time. Maybe I need to call that financial guy.*

The Day After

At work the next day, Richard sat preoccupied at his desk. Even with his promotion and catching the meth dealer, none of it mattered if he lost his family.

His boss, Lt. Davis, had him into his office just before lunch.

"Wanted to let you know about your pay increase now that the promotion to sergeant is official," the lieutenant said.

"Thanks," Richard said.

"You don't sound happy."

"It's just—" Richard hesitated. "Janet wasn't thrilled with the news. Things are kind of rough for us right now."

"Even though the money's better?"

"There never seems to be enough." Richard looked out the window at the precinct. Everyone milled around, doing the work he loved. Why couldn't this all work out?

"Hm," the lieutenant said. "I have a thought for you. Barb and I used to have money troubles, too, but then we got a handle on it. It's not that hard. You might just need some help."

Richard turned to him blankly. "Help?" he asked.

"Yeah, like a financial advisor. Ours got us out of a real hole."

Richard looked skeptical. "Don't those guys charge an arm and a leg?"

"Well, he wasn't cheap. He was Fee-Only."

"What does that mean?"

"It means you pay him a flat fee for his services. And I tell you, by the end, we were glad to pay our guy. He changed our lives."

Richard still wasn't buying it, and he didn't think his marital problems would be solved by some financial guru. But it was his boss talking, so he took the business card the lieutenant dug out of his desk drawer. The name on the card read, "Danny Venegas." "Thanks, I'll check it out," Richard said, as they walked together back to Richard's desk.

Richard had thought that morning about canceling the once-a-week lunch he had with his dad, but forgot to make the call before being called back into the lieutenant's office. There his dad was, joshing around with the other officers, when Richard returned to his desk.

"Hey, Mike, great to see you again," the lieutenant said, cuffing Richard's dad on the arm. Mike used to be on the force.

"Yeah, Davis, I remember when you were first out of the academy. Now here you're, promoting my son to sergeant." Mike looked proudly at Richard.

"He deserves it, he's a hard worker."

"Thanks," Richard said shortly. "Ready for lunch?"

He and his dad went down to the neighborhood diner. Richard was quiet, and Mike prattled on as he usually did. But it didn't mean he wasn't noticing Richard's mood. Once they settled at their table, Mike turned to him.

"What's on your mind?"

"It's just me and Janet. She's not happy with the promotion—"

"Uh, oh." Mike looked serious. "How bad is it?"

Richard shook his head.

"Son, don't let it get too far. Remember what happened to your mom and me."

"I know." Richard had lived through that divorce as a teenager. "I swore I'd never do that."

"But here you are, on the force, just like the old man." Mike gripped his shoulder. "You don't have someone else, do you? Does she?"

"No, Dad, it's not like that. Most of our problems have to do with money."

"Money? Oh, hell, that's the easy stuff."

Richard remembered the card in his pocket. "The lieutenant recommended a financial advisor."

Mike scoffed at this idea. "You don't need that kind of crap, someone coming in and telling you what to do. Just handle it yourself. Make her stop spending."

But Richard knew it wasn't all Janet's fault. "I don't know, Dad—"

"Listen, son, you gotta let her know who's in charge."

Richard didn't say it, but he thought, *Yeah, see how that worked for you.* His dad had never even made sergeant. "Thanks, we'll figure it out." He decided he'd check out Danny Venegas online when he got home.

A Different Experience

That night, Janet saw Richard hunched over the computer right after she gave Matthew his bath. After she snuggled the baby into his jammies, she carried him nonchalantly past her husband and glanced at the computer. Surprised, she saw the logo of the financial advisor her own lawyer had recommended.

"What are you working on?" she asked, alarmed suddenly that Richard had a divorce attorney of his own. They'd been frosty to each other since the fight the night before, but there had been no more arguing. In fact, they were hardly talking. Once Richard finally came home from his motorcycle ride, he'd slept in the guest room.

"It's this financial advisor my boss recommended," Richard said, frowning into the screen and not noticing Janet's sigh of relief. "I thought I'd check it out, but when I called him, all I got was a voicemail message to apply online."

When Richard had called Janet's uncle, the receptionist immediately transferred him. Roger was anxious to meet right away. But when Richard called Danny Venegas's number, there was only a recorded voice message with instructions that seemed very odd to Richard.

The recording explained that Danny accepted very few new clients, and in order to be considered they would need to complete and submit a lengthy application. Then Danny would review the application to determine if they were eligible for a one-hour orientation appointment.

Janet pulled up a chair, Matthew on her lap. "I think I've heard of that guy. Show me." She remembered what the lawyer had said about straightening out their financials before separating. Now was as good a time as any.

Richard glanced over at her as he pulled up the application. She didn't look mad—it was more like she was determined. But then he saw what had downloaded.

"Whoa," he said.

Janet squinted at the screen. "How long is that?"

"It's several pages to fill out to see if the guy will even meet with us." Richard clicked down the screens. "Then if he agrees to meet us, we have to pay him for the first meeting." He hit the print button. Several pages started spitting out.

Matthew squirmed in Janet's arms, and she rose to put him to bed. "I don't understand why it is so difficult," Janet said. "Why can't we just make an appointment?"

"According to his website, he only accepts clients he thinks will work well with him. He says the first meeting is to determine if each of us thinks we can work together as part of a long-term relationship."

"Sounds like a job interview," Janet said, discouraged.

"Or a marriage." That just slipped out. Richard gave Janet a sheepish look, but she rolled her eyes.

"Let me put Matthew to bed," she said, with that determined look on her face again. "We've got to figure this out."

The Application

Once Matthew was in bed, Richard and Janet tackled Danny's application.

It took over an hour, and involved searching through records and figuring things out they'd never had to think about before. This was no fun. And Janet was not in a joking mood. Every time Richard tried to lighten things up or show any affection, she'd tighten her lips and turn back to the application. He was afraid to ask if she was really thinking about divorce—that might become very unpleasant. Instead, they focused on their money situation.

One part of the application gave instruction on how to figure out their net worth. Both Richard and Janet had heard that term, but neither had ever actually figured it out. It was eye opening.

They filled in all the blank lines showing each of their assets and liabilities. On the left side of the form they listed everything they owned and how much it was worth. These were things like cars, the motorcycle, and bank account balances, and would have included their house if they didn't rent. The application also asked for investment and retirement accounts balances, for which they had very little.

On the right side they listed everything they owed money for, including any mortgage (which they didn't have), car notes, the motorcycle (again), and the worst thing—credit cards. Digging around for that information was irritating, and almost started them fighting again when they saw the results.

After they listed everything, they added up the left side and then subtracted the right side. Even though they'd had no idea what their net worth was when they started this exercise, it still turned out to be a very low number. This was the first time they knew for a fact how much money they would have if they sold everything they owned and paid off all of their bills, and it wasn't pretty.

Even Richard felt grim now. They started then on the essay-type questions. One, which took considerable time and thinking for Janet and Richard to answer, asked, "In order of importance, what are your three biggest financial concerns or problems?" And another asked, "Up to this point, what has prevented you from being able to solve those concerns or problems?"

Answering these and the rest of the questions on the application proved to be a stretch. Richard and Janet agreed their first and second concerns were insufficient money each month and excess credit card debt. However, they couldn't agree on the third, and decided to each list their own.

Richard listed their taxes as his third problem. He wasn't clear in his mind what the problem was, and he did not know if they were overpaying or not. In reality he was still upset that he couldn't take his hunting trip the prior year and probably wouldn't be able to that year, either. But he didn't bring this up to Janet.

Janet, however, listed retirement planning as her third item. She had always been worried that they weren't doing much of anything to plan for tomorrow, and now that she was thinking she might be a single mom, it seemed like they'd wasted all this time. Lumped in with this was Richard's lack of life insurance, but since the form asked them to prioritize the top three, and they already listed four, she decided that their lack of retirement planning ranked more important to her.

After they finished the forms and put the stamp on the envelope to mail it in, they both hoped they'd be able to get an appointment with Danny—but they didn't say this to each other. The instructions explained that Danny would review the application and they would be notified if they were qualified for the initial appointment.

The next few days had them in a weird space emotionally. They were still mad, especially Janet, but the very act of working together on the application and both wondering if they'd "made it" subtly made them feel like a team again. They began to have hope that maybe they could solve their money issues, even though they both had different motivations.

They waited anxiously, and exactly one week later they received a call from Danny's assistant.

Preliminary Appointment

Richard and Janet had no idea what to expect during their first meeting. Danny was already so different than Janet's uncle. To start, the application process and having to send an initial payment was new. Then, being invited to Danny's home for their first meeting was very different. Danny's assistant told them to bring their last three years of tax returns with them.

They almost felt like this was an audition of some kind. Richard especially was secretly worried he didn't know enough about money for Danny to be interested in working with them. On the way over, Richard told Janet about his meeting with her uncle and prepared her for what they could probably expect from Danny. Richard said that within about ten minutes of his meeting with her uncle, he tried to get him to sign up for the insurance investment. They agreed before going to the appointment that they would talk about it privately before signing up for anything.

Their GPS took them to a quiet Santa Barbara neighborhood, with spacious but not huge houses and understated, simple lawns. The address turned out to be a normal, two-story house with an older model

Lexus in the driveway. *It's not even as nice as Stephanie's place*, Janet thought. *How successful can this guy be?*

Danny, a middle-aged man who radiated calm and wellbeing, met them at the door and welcomed them in. He wore khakis and a light-blue, collared T-shirt. "Thank you for coming," he said. "We can talk in the office, but if you prefer we can sit on the back patio in the garden. It would be a shame to waste such a beautiful day locked inside."

The back yard was bigger than they expected, and comfortably arranged with tables and chairs and a badminton net that had seen some wear. A summer breeze stirred through the trees lining the property. *No pool, though*, Janet thought. She and Richard were surprised by how casual Danny was, but it was nice that he made them feel so at ease.

After they sat down, Danny said, "During the next hour I'm going to ask you a lot of questions to find out if I can help you or not. Then if I think we will be a good fit, I will explain how I work. Meanwhile I want you to ask any question you may have so you can decide if this is right for you. Do you have any questions before we get started?"

Both Janet and Richard had a lot of questions, but neither knew where to begin. They replied in unison, "Nope."

"Great. I read your application very carefully, but let's begin by you telling me what brought you here today."

Richard winced and looked over at Janet, who was staring off into the garden, her lips tight.

"We want to get on better footing financially," Richard started, but Janet cut him off.

"My divorce attorney said it's better get your finances in order before you split up." Janet's tone was flat. She glared over at Danny.

Danny's eyebrows rose. "I see," he said slowly. He glanced at Richard, who looked shell-shocked but didn't argue with her. "Who's your attorney?" Danny asked. When Janet named her, Danny's lips twitched like he was hiding a smile. "I've heard of her," he said casually. "She does family law also, doesn't she?"

Janet nodded.

"Well, she knows what she's talking about." Danny drew in a breath. "All right," he said. "let's just see how far we can get with the basics."

Danny started with specific questions like, "What experience do you have with investing?" and some very broad philosophical questions such as, "What would it take to live the life you've always wanted?" Some of these questions were things neither Richard nor Janet had ever considered, and they had to think about them. Richard kept answering with the word "we," as in "We'd like to..." but Janet kept all her answers as "I." Danny didn't challenge them in either direction.

Then Danny went into some of the specifics of their finances and reviewed their past three years' tax returns. Richard talked about his hunting trip and how disappointed he was that he couldn't go. He expected a financial advisor to counsel him to save his money and wait until retirement for such extravagant vacations, but to the contrary, Danny said, "Those types of things are important to a happy and fulfilling life. We can budget to make sure that stuff happens as part of the financial planning process." Janet rolled her eyes.

At the end of the hour, Danny said, "I think we could work well together, so I'm willing to take you on as clients."

Richard was surprised. "But we don't know anything!"

"If you knew everything already, you wouldn't need me," Danny said. "I'm looking for clients who are genuinely interested in improving their lives. I could tell from your application that you both put significant effort into getting the information together. Also, your responses today make me think we'd be a good match as far as my being able to help you. It might take some time, but I'm confident you can make rapid progress toward your financial goals."

"Is that it?" Richard asked surprised.

"Yes, that's it," Danny smiled. "If you want, we can schedule an appointment to meet again, or you can go home and talk about it and then schedule an appointment if you decide you'd like to work with me."

Janet was impressed at the low-key sales approach, and it was good to know Danny thought they were good candidates for achieving their financial goals. "Let's schedule an appointment while we're here," she suggested.

"That's a good idea, because my schedule fills up fast. Then you can talk it over, and I can answer any questions you have when we meet again," Danny said.

They scheduled the appointment for later in the week.

The Decision

Janet and Richard drove in stunned silence for a few blocks after their meeting.

"Well, what do you think?" Janet finally asked.

"That sure wasn't what I expected," Richard answered. "What I went in thinking we needed is not what I think we need now."

Janet nodded in spite of herself. "I felt the same way."

"He didn't even talk about investments or try to sign us up for anything. You and I talked almost the entire time, and he listened. In my meeting with your uncle, I didn't say much, and it seemed like he was trying to sell me something the entire time."

"Danny asked some tough questions, though," Janet replied.

"So do you want to work with him?" Richard asked.

"Do you?"

Richard thought it over before answering. He didn't want to seem eager to get divorced, but that was about the last thing he wanted to bring up—he knew they'd have to talk about it eventually, just not today. The prospect of finally figuring out how money worked would be good either way. "Yeah, I do. I think he understands our situation."

"All right, let's do it," Janet said. It felt like the smartest decision they'd made in a while.

Then Richard remembered something. "Wait—we never asked him how much he costs."

"I hadn't even thought of that," Janet said. She bit her lip. She hoped they could afford it. The same old thing wasn't working.

"I'm sure we'll find out next time we meet," Richard said.

Turning Point

At the next meeting, Danny explained how his consulting contract worked. He went through it line by line and made sure Janet and Richard understood everything.

Then he quoted his fee. Janet and Richard were both shocked. They had known it wouldn't be cheap, but they were still surprised. But Danny explained how a quick look at their taxes had shown him already how they could regain almost a third of his fee by filing amendments. That, in combination with his patient overview of the contract and their gut instinct that he was trustworthy, encouraged them to get out the pens. When they signed, they both knew it was the right decision.

The first thing they agreed to tackle was their taxes. In their first meeting, Danny had noted that their previous three tax returns were all done by different tax preparers. One year Janet had done them herself, and two other years were with two different accountants. Danny pointed out discrepancies in all three returns and suggested there appeared to be some mistakes and neglected tax deductions.

"It's very common," Danny explained. "When you spend so little time with a tax preparer it's hard for them to understand your entire life circumstances, and they can overlook valid tax deductions. The more often you change tax preparers, the less the preparer can get to know your unique situation."

Danny brought out some forms he'd already filled out to amend the past three tax returns and correct the errors. These changes would net them a tax refund for one-third of his fee. Danny told them it didn't always happen so nicely, but once in a while it did, and they lucked out. Things were looking better already.

Their next assignment before the next meeting was to assemble what would be needed for the current year's return. Janet and Richard went home and spent a fair amount of time digging up receipts and figuring out all of the expenses that they never knew were valid tax deductions. There were many unreimbursed expenses that Richard had as a police officer that he hadn't claimed, and Janet hadn't known she could deduct the miles on her car that she drove for work. Janet was also considered an independent contractor and had dedicated space in their home for her office. This allowed them to legally deduct a significant portion of their utility bills.

Janet and Richard managed to keep the peace until their next meeting with Danny, mostly because Janet was excruciatingly polite. Richard hated it, but it was better than fighting. He gave her space and kept sleeping in the guest room.

Budgeting

"It's good to see you both again," Danny said to Janet and Richard at their next appointment.

After Danny was finished projecting their tax return, Janet and Richard were happy to see they would get a large tax refund that year, especially after they were so afraid they might have to pay. Danny explained that by taking the legal tax deductions that they had been overlooking, they would be able to save a substantial amount of money.

Between the amended tax returns and the current year's tax refund, they had already received enough to pay half of Danny's fee. Janet was stunned; it was always a thrill to find free money. She almost turned to Richard and smiled, and had to stop herself. Richard was already mentally planning his hunting trip, but before he even said anything, Danny suggested they not spend the money just yet.

"Today," Danny said, "we'll talk about budgeting."

"Oh, that sounds like fun," Janet said.

"I know—budgeting can feel like dieting," Danny said. "In theory they both work, but it's the implementation that makes both dieting and budgeting almost worthless. The key for both is not to have strict and impossible rules to follow, but instead to create an environment where negative influences are removed."

"Like one partner spending too much money?" Janet said.

Richard bit his tongue. *Janet's the one with all the shoes,* he thought.

Danny didn't skip a beat. "Sure, both partners and any kids in the family who are spending money have to be on the same page. But there are some ways to make it easier. For almost twenty years, I kept track of all of my expenditures with software programs, and I used to recommend my clients do the same. Eventually I realized that very few people are disciplined enough to keep these records, but more importantly, merely keeping track of purchases does little to modify behavior."

"At least we'd know where the money's going, though," Richard said. "All those little purchases, even if things are on sale, can add up as much as big ticket items."

Janet tapped her foot impatiently.

"Right," Danny continued smoothly. "But let's get specific. Maybe I review my annual expenses and find that on average I spend $300 per month eating out. In reality, this tells me nothing. For some families this is outrageous, and for others it's insignificant. It also doesn't tell you how much value you or your family places on dining out. Perhaps the $300 is a frivolous waste of money that you'd prefer spending elsewhere. Or maybe going out to restaurants is the only time your family gets to spend quality time together without the distraction of the television, work and phones."

Janet frowned. "So you also have to figure out what's important to you."

Danny nodded. "In this case, the monthly $300 may be the most important thing you spend money on. The point is that the arbitrary numbers that come from reviewing historical expenditures do little to prioritize your values or modify future spending. This surprises most people, but the system that works best for my clients is to ignore complicated record keeping systems, except for businesses of course, and instead to use a system of multiple bank accounts and cash."

Danny put a blank sheet of paper on the table in front of them.

"First," he said, making notes of steps to take, "determine what your mandatory monthly expenses are, such as your mortgage, car payments, and utility bills."

"I know all those," Janet said. "I handle them every month." She jotted them right down on the paper. Richard was impressed.

"Excellent," Danny said. "You're ahead of the game just knowing these things. What you'll do next is assign a checking account specifically for these bills. Have all income from all sources deposited into this checking account."

"We've already set up a direct deposit through my job," Richard said.

"It's becoming common now, which makes it very easy," Danny agreed. "Janet should do that too, if possible. Set up automated monthly payments to cover each of your mandatory expenses. If you're not having your monthly savings and retirement contributions automatically deducted from your paycheck, have these funds also drafted from this account as well. This makes savings mandatory and a priority on par with paying the rent instead of waiting to see if there is anything left over at the end of the month."

"Savings?" Janet looked doubtful. "Retirement contributions? We don't have much of that."

"We'll get to it," Danny assured her. "The more we can automate all the regular payments, the closer we'll get to the savings goals. Next, set up a second checking account to pay your discretionary expenses. A set amount will be automatically transferred to this account once we've determined a good monthly amount for you. From this account you can pay for bills that are more optional or flexible, such as groceries, cable, dry cleaning, and entertainment."

"How are groceries discretionary?" Richard asked.

"Good question," Danny answered. "Clients often think many of these things are not flexible, such as groceries. But they are because you have many options that range from steak and lobster to freeze-dried noodles. Using this method allows you to moderate your spending within this account based on how much is in there. If there is a plenty of money, then steak may be an option, but if the account balance is running low, peanut butter and jelly may be the menu for a couple of days. If at the end of each month you regularly have money left over, you may decide to decrease the money coming from account one to account two, which will allow more money to go to credit card payments or investments."

"What about all those things we pay once a year like insurance and stuff?" Janet asked.

"Create account number three," Danny said.

"You really like bank accounts don't you?" Richard said joking.

Danny laughed and continued, "This account will be used to make payments for large annual expenses like you mentioned, Janet, and later, can be where emergency funds are held. Taxes and auto, home, and life insurance are often due annually instead of monthly. If these are not planned in advance, they often get paid for with credit cards."

Danny drew a little chart on the page in front of him and asked Richard and Janet to fill in the numbers. "To fund account three, you first add up all of the annual expenses and divide the total by twelve. Each month you will set up an automatic bank transfer from account one to account three for the monthly amount."

The chart looked like this:

Auto Insurance	$1,200
Renter's Insurance	$2,000
Annual Vacation	$2,400
Etc.	

They totaled up all the annual expenses and divided this by twelve to get the amount that needed to be transferred into this account each month.

Danny then asked, "Are there any things either of you'd like to spend less on?"

"Do you mean like expensive coffee? I like going to Starbucks, but I probably spend more there than I should," Richard answered.

"You're not the first client who has mentioned how much they spend on fancy coffees or restaurants," Danny said. "There is no right or wrong amount that you should spend on any luxury and no financial advisor should ever impose his or her values on you, but if you feel that way, here is a tip that works very well.

"As I said earlier, it's possible that eating out or getting coffee is an important part of your life and you'd prefer to cut something else out when money gets tight. But if you do want to limit spending in a specific area, the simplest way is to set a weekly limit. Then make a cash withdrawal each week and put the money in your purse or wallet. Once you've spent the money, then you're done until the next week."

Janet wasn't sure. "But what about credit cards? We could always just whip one out if we run out of cash."

Danny nodded. "You'd have to be disciplined. Some of my clients take their credit cards and freeze them—literally—to keep from using them."

"You mean, put them in the freezer?" Richard laughed.

"You'd be surprised how effective that is. They're there if you need them, but it takes awhile for them to thaw out." Danny grinned when he saw they both were amused by this idea. "Now, back to the cash. If you want to limit your lunch and coffee break expenses to $100 per week, simply withdraw that much from the bank each week. Having this limited amount will help you make better choices when you know you only have so much to work with. This is so simple, yet it works amazingly well at limiting spending and removing any guilt or anxiety you may have previously felt when spending money."

Danny then summarized it all with bullet points on the sheet of paper. "You will have three separate bank accounts. Deposit income from all sources into account one. Account one will be used to pay mandatory expenses such as rent, car payments, and contributions to savings. Then automatically transfer a fixed amount of money from account one to account two each month for discretionary expenses. Transfer another fixed amount monthly to account three to pay for large and/or annual expenses. Finally, withdraw a predetermined amount of cash at fixed intervals from account one for discretionary spending you want to regulate."

Danny finished by saying, "The more automated this system is the more effective it will be. With today's technology of online bill payments, direct deposit, and automatic bank transfers, most of this system can be completely automated, which helps guarantee your success. This system works because it doesn't force you to track your expenses. Instead it lets you decide what is most important to you and adjust your spending accordingly. You never have to worry about running out of money for the critical bills. It's a way of budgeting without the headaches of a budget."

Richard and Janet were both nodding to themselves.

"I think I get it," Janet said.

"Yeah, me too," Richard responded. "We can set this all up when we get home."

"Terrific," Danny said. "Why not take a few weeks to get used to that system? When you're comfortable with it, we'll do our next meeting. Get ready—you'll be bringing in all your credit card statements, so we can start to tackle that. In fact, that's the first of the Five Fundamentals of financial success."

"There are only five?" Richard joked. "Should be a snap."

Getting Set Up

Richard charged full steam ahead into setting up all the bank accounts Danny had recommended. He'd been impressed with how simple Danny made managing their monthly expenditures sound, and he embraced it wholeheartedly. It felt good to be doing something concrete to solve their problems, even if it was only financial and not marital.

While Richard did that, Janet spent some time going over old bills and figuring out how much to put where each month. It made her think about what life would be like if she had to do this on her own. She knew it wouldn't be easy, but she thought, *It's better than parenting with an absent partner.*

That night they were both ready with their parts of the process, Richard came home at a reasonable hour and, after putting Matthew to bed, he and Janet huddled over the computer to set up the automatic payments with their online banking system. They even drew up a flow chart to make it clear to themselves where the money was coming from, where it would land in account one, and then how it would be disbursed to the other accounts.

"Hey, there's some left over," Richard said, surprised. It had seemed like every month they'd never had anything left.

"Well, we haven't figured out how much to put toward credit card debt," Janet said. "We've got to get a handle on that."

"Danny said that would be our next meeting."

Janet nodded. "But we also have to determine how much cash to take out each week as our pocket money for things like lunch and coffee. I'm not sure, but I think I need at least $100."

Richard wanted to be agreeable, but that seemed high to him. "You sure you need that much? Every week?"

She turned on him, exasperated. "You try to make things work with taking clients to lunch, getting things for Matthew, and still trying to stay sane!" The "staying sane" category included things like pedicures, but she didn't say that out loud.

"All right, all right," Richard said. "I'll take $100, too, and we'll see how it goes. I'll go get it in the morning and drop yours off with you before you leave for work."

Janet stiffened up. "I can get my own."

"But then that's two withdrawals," Richard objected.

"So what?"

"I think we should keep track of it closely, so there aren't a bunch of withdrawals, that's all." For some reason, Richard felt stubborn on this point. Maybe it was because he wanted to think of them as a team rather than two separate people.

Janet, on the other hand, thought otherwise. "I don't want you handing out money to me, like it's my allowance," she said. *That would be too much like Dad.*

Richard didn't understand. "That's not what I meant."

"Whatever. Why don't I get it all out, and give you yours?"

She was testing his need for control, but he actually didn't have any. "That's fine," Richard agreed immediately. "I just didn't want you to get stuck with an extra errand."

Still frustrated, Janet stood up suddenly. "I'm going to bed. Good night."

She left him there, his head spinning a little. Richard logged out of the bank website and thought, *Well, at least we agreed on something.*

The Five Fundamentals

A few weeks went by. They started with each getting $100 cash on Mondays, but by Friday, Janet would be out. A lot of the expenses that were work related but not deductible, like gas for the car or quick lunches on the road, she used to put on the credit card. Now, the cash had to cover it. She also noticed she was the one paying for the many little things that Matthew needed, since she was the primary caregiver. It didn't seem fair that it all had to come out of her pocket.

But when she brought it up to Richard when they were on their way to their next appointment with Danny, he wasn't that sympathetic. He secretly enjoyed having proof that he spent less than she did. He knew he wasn't being the better man, but he couldn't help rubbing it in a little.

"See," he said. "I told you all those little things add up."

"It's not like you have that many expenses," Janet retorted. "I see how you've started making a brown bag lunch, which comes out of the grocery money, just so you can say you spent less of the cash."

"You could do that, too."

Janet exploded. "Excuse me? I'm taking care of Matthew, running around in my car all day meeting clients, trying to juggle everything, and you want me to make my own lunch? So I can eat it sitting in my car in some parking lot? You at least get to eat with all your buddies."

Richard let her rant as they pulled into Danny's driveway. She was still in a snit when they sat down at Danny's patio table and Richard pulled out the credit card statements.

It didn't take a genius to notice Janet's tension, and Danny was pretty damn smart.

"So," Danny asked cautiously, "how's it going?"

"Oh, *fine*," Janet snapped.

"We set up all the accounts," Richard said hastily. "And started with the cash system."

Janet snorted.

Danny looked from one to the other before asking, "Is that working for you guys?"

"No, it's not," Janet said. "It's not a fair system."

Danny's face showed his surprise. "My system has been called many things," he said, "but 'unfair' is a new one. How is it unfair?"

"We each get the same amount of money," Janet said, "but Richard always winds up with more than I do."

"Oh," Danny said in realization. "It's not necessarily the case that you both should have the exact same amount. You probably have different cash flow needs during the week."

Janet gave him a look of pure gratitude. "Thank you!" she said.

Danny glanced at Richard, who was looking innocently at the awning overhead. Danny grinned. "It could be that you should adjust those amounts depending on what each of you needs," Danny said. "If Janet has more expenses out of pocket because of Matthew or her work, that should be figured in."

"So I don't have to ask Richard for more money?"

Danny shook his head. "No, you'll just wind up fighting."

Janet and Richard looked at each other.

Danny said, "You should each figure out how much you need, and get that amount, adjusting as necessary."

Janet waited for Richard to argue the point, but all he said was, "Right." He'd known all along their set-up wasn't entirely fair, but he'd enjoyed feeling like a money master. Now, it was easy to agree to change. "Janet should get more of the cash every week."

A smile lit up Janet's face before she could stop it. She tried to hide it behind her hand, but Richard saw it anyway. It gave him a jolt he hadn't felt in a while. They couldn't meet each other's eyes for a full ten minutes.

Danny let them savor the moment, then explained the purpose of their meeting that day—starting on the Five Fundamentals.

Fundamental #1: Credit Cards

This meeting, Danny explained, would be a bit different than the others they'd had because it would be more educational. He explained it was time to lay the ground work for everything else they were going to do.

"Almost all financial problems stem from not following these Five Fundamentals I'll be introducing to you," Danny explained. "It'll take several meetings to cover all five. They serve as a starting point for everyone, and we will work on each one thoroughly before moving on to the next."

Danny pulled out a piece of paper and started a list:

1. Pay off all credit cards and consumer debt

"Oh good luck with that," Richard said, after reading Danny's words.

But Janet became earnest. "No, we've got to get a handle on that." She leaned forward, fully engaged.

Danny nodded. "Credit card debt can be a real problem. By definition, when using credit cards and not paying the entire balance each month, you're spending more than you have. That can lead to stress and frustration for the whole family. It isn't the trips or the clothes that causes this anxiety; it's going deeper into debt that does. Not all debt is bad, but consumer debt causes a lot of stress for many Americans."

"Some debt can work as a powerful tool to leverage your assets and protect you against inflation. The most common example of good debt is a 30-year fixed mortgage on your primary residence. However, the majority of debt does not offer the same benefits as a mortgage. For financial solvency, paying off credit cards must become a priority."

Janet and Richard were following him closely, so Danny decided to fill them in on his personal philosophy. "The problem with consumer debt," he said, "is that you're committing to paying in the future for experiences you had in the past. The joy or benefits from those purchases typically don't last as long as the ongoing payments."

"What do you mean by consumer debt exactly?" Janet asked.

"I'm talking about goods and services that have a short life span or decrease in value the moment you buy them," Danny answered.

"You mean like going out to dinner," Richard said.

"Right," Danny said. "Although eating out can be fun, the value doesn't outlast the time you're paying for it."

Richard tried to put this in more simplified language. "So if I have to pay for it longer than it lasts, it's not okay to finance it?"

Danny nodded. "That's a good way to look at it. In the mortgage example, your home provides ongoing use and pleasure while typically increasing in value—at least over the long run. The debt on your credit cards, however, increases with time because of high interest rates, and rarely do the things you buy with the credit cards maintain their value.

"A very simple way to measure good debt verses bad debt is if the item you're purchasing on credit is likely to increase in value and/or provide you income, it's probably good debt. But if it will only depreciate in value resulting in more debt than the item is worth, it's probably bad debt and not a good idea to put on a credit card."

"Well, I don't know," Janet said with some doubt in her voice.

Danny didn't understand her objection. "What do you mean, Janet?"

But she was joking. "Some of my shoes are pretty damn valuable!" The guys laughed. This whole session had put her in a good mood.

Five Steps to Killing Consumer Debt

Danny walked them through the five steps of killing consumer debt, making a list of them on another sheet of paper.

Step 1) Inventory consumer debt

"The first step is to take inventory of all of your consumer debt," Danny explained. "This includes all bank and store credit cards, lines of credit and home equity lines or second mortgages that were used to buy consumer goods or pay off previous credit card balances."

"We only have credit cards," Janet said.

"That's good, it makes it simpler," Danny said. "Let's list each credit card along with the balance, and minimum monthly payments. Add up all of the debt and total the monthly minimum payments."

Richard and Janet rifled through all the statements, found the numbers, and wrote them on the paper.

Step 2) Evaluate causes of debt

"The next step is the time for a bit of honest self-analysis," Danny said. "You have to evaluate why you make the purchases to begin with. Frankly, the reason we usually go into debt is to overcome some unhappiness in our life. We use debt to live a life we really can't afford."

Janet bit her lip, as Richard said, "There is a lot of truth to that. But sometimes we can't avoid getting in debt, like in an emergency."

"Well," said Danny, "let's look at the items in the statements."

The current month was pretty trim, since they'd come so close to their limits. But looking back over prior statements, Danny pointed out multitudes of little purchases, along with the habitual electronic gadget for Richard or spa visit for Janet.

"You see how you got these things months ago," Danny said, "but you're still paying for them? Rarely is consumer debt used to pay for some catastrophic expense like medical bills. It usually gets bigger because we spend too much trying to be happy and don't plan for emergencies with insurance and savings."

This was an aha moment for Janet. "I think I get it," she said. "Those spa visits were nice, but the relaxation doesn't last nearly as long as the tension from the debt."

"Exactly," Danny said. "Think about the things you've used credit for: vacations, cars, eating out, etc. All of those are luxuries, including the car. Do you need the car you drive, or is it possible you could have gotten by with something less expensive?

"Do I really need that motorcycle?" Richard said hypothetically. Janet turned to him in surprise, and he stared back at her. "Did I just say that out loud?"

She laughed, and he looked pleased with himself.

Danny then threw a big idea at them. "Ask yourself if the amount of monthly payments you're forced to pay to your credit cards makes you more or less happy than the original unhappiness you were trying to overcome when buying all of that stuff on credit."

Janet and Richard's brows both knit as they tried to do the math on that statement. "That's an intense question when you think about it," Richard said.

"More often than not," Danny continued, "the debt and burden of monthly payments leads to more stress than the short term happiness the purchase provided. But if that doesn't give you enough motivation to pay off your debt, we can twist the knife a little."

"Uh oh," Janet said. "Here it comes."

"For some more motivation," Danny said, "take your total monthly minimum credit card payments and ask yourself what else you could be doing with that money."

He made some notes on the paper. "For example," he continued, "it looks like your minimum credit card payments are about $860 each month. Imagine instead using that money to hire a housekeeper and never having to clean the house again. What if you saved $200 of that each month to go on an amazing family vacation?"

"Or what about something even bigger?" Richard asked, "like working fewer hours, spending more time together, or doing our hobbies?"

"That does hit home," Janet said. "There is a lot I'd rather do with the money I pay for my credit cards."

Danny nodded again. "Usually when it's laid out like this, it's easy to agree the material objects or restaurant meals you bought weren't worth the monthly payments you're paying for an eternity."

Step 3) Set the date

Danny then moved right to step three. "The prior step is intentionally designed to be painful. Its purpose is to provide the motivation that will let you dig deep and get those things paid off. You'll need a burning desire to pay off credit card debt because it's hard to do. Step two provides the motivation to pay them off. Once you've got that motivation, setting a concrete date is the only way to make it happen. As good old Antoine de Saint-Exupery said..."

"Who's he?" Richard cut in.

"He wrote *The Little Prince*," Janet offered. Richard was surprised at her literary knowledge, but she explained, "We got it for Matthew as a shower present."

Danny laughed. "Right. He said, 'A goal without a plan is just a wish.' Think about it. In order to make your wish of paying off your credit card debt come true, you need a clearly defined plan, and that means a deadline."

"How do you set a date? That seems complicated," Richard said.

"It not too hard," Danny answered. "Take the figures from step one along with the average interest rate and plug them into a debt calculator. There are free ones on the Internet, if we type 'debt calculator' into a search engine. Play around with the numbers to discover how soon you can be debt-free at various sized monthly payments. Pick a monthly payment you can afford, set a date, and stick to it."

"Can we do it right now?" Janet asked eagerly. Somehow, she wanted to know just how long this would take.

"Of course." Danny opened his laptop, and soon they were clicking away. The final result, while not in the immediate future, was a lot closer than either Richard of Janet had imagined.

Step 4) Prioritize the payoffs

"The next step is what will keep you going," Danny explained. "First, despite what the debt calculator said, now that we have the best total monthly payment, we can ignore the credit card interest rates. Emotionally, it's best to take the card with the smallest balance and focus on it first. Make the minimum monthly payments to each of the others, and put all the rest toward paying off that card with the smallest balance."

He continued, "Attack that card with everything you have until the balance is gone. You can even take it a step further. If you get a bonus at work, use it to pay that card down. If you can sell some junk in a garage sale, send that money to that card, too.

"Quickly your smallest credit card balance will be zero, and then you can shift all that money to the next smallest balance. This system is amazing because it works on your emotional level. Each credit card that is paid off is like a small victory and inspires you to keep going. At the same time, as each is paid off it frees up more money for the next card."

"It almost sounds fun!" Janet said.

"Especially if you celebrate each time you knock one down." Danny referred to their list of balances on the page. "With your credit cards, here's what I'd do."

Card A: $3,200 balance, 19% interest, minimum $128
Card B: $7,000 balance, 5.5% interest, minimum $280
Card C: $2,200 balance, 10% interest, minimum $88
Card D: $9,100 balance, 12% interest, minimum $364

"Mathematically it makes sense to attack credit card A first because of the higher interest rate. But paying off credit cards is an emotional battle so we have to focus on that," Danny explained. "In this example, using your debt calculator, you determined you can pay off all your debt in a reasonable amount of time with a $1,200 monthly payment. Set automatic monthly minimum payments to cards A, B, and D and set an automatic payment to C for the remainder of the $1,200."

"That puts things on auto pilot, but you still need to aggressively attack card C with any extra cash you have. Quickly, credit card C will be paid off. Then divert all your effort to card A. This works amazingly well because you will see progress fast."

Step 5) Commitment

Janet and Richard were looking impressed—and hopeful—when Danny moved on to the final step.

"All you need to get rid of all this debt is to make a commitment to pay them off at all costs," he said. "For single people, it's easier, but even married couples can do this if both are equally committed."

"I think this will work," Janet said, as Richard nodded.

Danny jumped right on that. "Can you commit to it right now?" he asked.

The "c" word—commitment. Janet and Richard looked at each other. They felt like they were getting married all over again.

"I do," Richard said, and Janet smiled.

Fundamental #2:
Save at Least 10%

T hings went well for Janet and Richard for a couple days. They went home from Danny's and launched their "pay down the credit cards" strategy. It felt great to send off those first payments, especially the big one to start obliterating card C. Janet came close to asking Richard to come back to their bedroom, but something still held her back.

Then the police department got busy with a round of narcotics busts, and Richard's hours skyrocketed. He felt good because it meant extra cash for getting out of debt even quicker, but he wasn't there to see how lonely and stressed Janet became. In her darkest moments, she again began thinking about going at it alone. At least she'd be doing things on her own terms.

They'd barely seen each other for the several days leading up to their next appointment with Danny. In fact, to Janet, it seemed like visiting Danny was the only time they ever did see each other. Her day had been filled with phone calls and appointments, running around with Matthew to play groups and to her mom's, and turning down lunch with

Stephanie because she had to get groceries. Stephanie had a thing or two to say about that!

Janet was tense and quiet on the ride over to Danny's. Richard's head was filled with work details, though, and he didn't notice.

When Danny asked them how things were going, Richard launched right into how great he felt about paying down those credit cards. He went into detail about how he and Janet had set up the payments and dived right in. Janet nodded quietly in support. She was happy about getting rid of their debt, too, but her day had been so stressed she found it hard to show much enthusiasm.

Danny redirected them to the next Fundamental. He took out their sheet of paper and wrote #2:

1. Pay off all credit cards and consumer debt
2. Save at least 10% of all your income

Janet's eyebrows rose. "Ten percent?"

"That seems like an awful lot of money," Richard said with a bit of concern.

Danny explained, "Eventually I want you to save at least 10% of all earnings, before taxes, for the rest of your working lives. There may be times when saving more is necessary, but this is the minimum goal. However, it's often a stretch for people to immediately jump to a full 10% of their salary, so it works best if you ease into it. The other part that makes this possible is that you pay yourself first before you write checks for any other bills. This has become a cliché in the personal finance business, but that's because it works so well."

To Janet, this just sounded like it would add to the stress level. "We're already struggling to make ends meet as it is, so I don't know how we will be able to save that much right now," she said.

Danny nodded with understanding. "In the beginning, it's more important to create the habit of saving than to worry about the actual percentage you're saving." Because Janet and Richard were just beginning, Danny proposed they start by saving 5% of their income. "By having the money automatically deducted from your paychecks, you will quickly get used to it and eventually increase the amount until you reach the 10% level. For now, you won't notice the 5% savings very much, especially after what we're about to do as an important step for Fundamental #2—tax planning."

Tax Planning

"How do our taxes relate to saving 10% of our income?" Janet asked.

"And I thought we already handled our taxes," Richard said.

"Let's get started, and I'll explain," Danny said. "We've cleaned up mistakes of the last few years and have gotten this year off to a good start, but we need to make some adjustments that will work into the future."

Danny said that it's far more difficult to save money on taxes while completing the tax return. Most people mistakenly assume it's up to the tax preparer to find tax savings when completing the forms. However, the real savings comes from aggressive tax planning before it's time to complete the return.

"The return is merely documenting what's already happened, so it's often too late to make changes," Danny said. "When planning ahead of time, you can proactively take steps that will save you lots of money on taxes."

Danny pulled out a report he'd prepared for them using the information from their past tax returns along with their current income statements to estimate how much they would owe in taxes the following year. When Danny told them how much their total state and federal taxes would be, Janet and Richard were both shocked.

"I don't understand," Richard asked. "We've never had to pay taxes before. We always get a refund. Why will we have to pay so much this year?"

"Many people believe that same thing," Danny said, "but in fact, Richard, you have paid almost this much every year. You just don't notice it because it's deducted a little at a time from each paycheck."

"Oh, I see," Janet said, relieved. "You don't mean that we will have to write a check for that amount, but that's how much they will take out in total from all of our paychecks."

"Right," Danny said. "What's important about this is if we can lower the amount that is withheld from your paycheck to the legal minimum, that's a lot more money in your pocket."

Richard frowned. "So we're going to reduce the withholding?"

"That would be like getting a pay raise," Janet said.

Danny nodded. "We're going to give you a pay raise that will be legally funded by Uncle Sam. Isn't this a great country?"

They discussed different ways they could save money using retirement accounts while also saving money on taxes. Richard had no idea, for example, that if he contributed $100 to his retirement account, his paycheck would only be $63 less because of his particular tax bracket. It was amazing how they could begin saving money at a fraction of the cost.

At the end of that day's meeting, Danny printed out new forms to give to Richard's employer to adjust his tax withholding. Danny showed how even with money now coming directly out of Richard's paycheck for retirement, the new payroll withholding would let him take more money home each time. This seemed unbelievable to Janet, so she asked, "How is it possible that we're now contributing money directly to a retirement account and still taking home more money?"

"We've made a bunch of little changes," Danny answered, "but I'll start with the bad news." He explained that they had now reduced their expected tax refund to zero. "Many people like getting surprise tax refunds, but it's better to have that money each month and to put it to use rather than waiting until the end of the year for a surprise."

Then he explained how they were saving money by taking more tax deductions that they had been overlooking and by lowering their taxable income by contributing to their retirement accounts. "All of these factors combined resulted in more money in your pocket while saving," Danny explained.

"That's just amazing. I wish we had done it ages ago," Janet said.

"Yes, it's nice when it works out this well. The key to making this work, though, is to immediately direct that extra money to something important. Otherwise it's tempting to spend it frivolously," Danny said.

"Like on a hunting trip?" Janet said sarcastically. Richard's grin was a little stilted.

"I haven't forgotten that trip," Danny said. "We haven't discussed the extra money from your tax withholdings yet."

"Are you serious?" Richard asked surprised. "I thought you'd suggest we save it."

"Often with lump sums and extra income like this I suggest you do a little of both," Danny responded. "If all you do is save for tomorrow and don't have any fun today, you'll lose motivation. Besides, what's the point if you can't have any fun today?"

Richard liked this idea, but Janet protested. "Why should he have all the fun?" she said. "I'd rather pay down debt than spend more."

"What would be fun for you, Janet?" Danny asked.

This hit her by surprise, and to the horror of the men, her eyes teared up.

Janet's Goals

"What I need," Janet said, while Richard and Danny braced themselves, "is maybe some time off. Maybe once a week."

Relieved, Richard jumped right on this. "I can do that," he said.

She shrugged at him. "Don't do me any favors."

"No, Matthew is my son, too. If you need time to yourself I'll do more of the parenting."

But even this didn't help. Janet didn't want to sob in front of the two men, so she sniffed into a tissue from her purse. Something crystallized for her in that moment, and she looked up with a new intensity.

"What I really want," she said, "is to be able to stay home to raise my child."

Danny waited for Richard to respond to that one.

Richard was stunned for a moment. "That's huge," he finally said.

"I know it," Janet said, discouraged. "I know it's impossible. But it's what I want more than anything."

"Oh, honey—" Richard started, but Danny cleared his throat.

When they both looked at him, Danny said, "If you want it more than anything, it can be done. The whole point of financial planning is to be able to shape the life you want."

Janet wiped her eyes. "What do you mean?"

"Look, money is no mystery," Danny said. "It comes in and it goes out. All financial planning means is taking control of how it flows. You can make it do whatever you want once you know what the goal is." He turned to Richard. "If you and Janet can agree that this is a long-term goal, say within a few years, we can definitely make that happen."

Janet turned to Richard with hope in her eyes, but she bit her lip when she saw his expression. He just couldn't see it yet. How could they live without her income? But Richard wanted to make his wife happy.

"Do you really think that's possible?" he asked Danny.

"Anything is possible," Danny replied with assurance. "You just have to commit." He saw Richard was still troubled. "Let's put this on the agenda for a future meeting. Today, we'll finish up deciding how to allocate the additional money from the lower tax withholding from your paychecks."

Richard liked the sound of that. Together, the three of them discussed options. Janet suggested the idea of using it pay down their credit cards. Richard wanted to lobby for his hunting trip, but that sounded lame now that he knew what Janet's goal was. Danny brought up the idea of starting an emergency fund.

Danny said, "There are many right answers when you have competing priorities such as credit cards, an emergency fund, staying home, and pleasure things like the trip. You have to weigh the high interest fees of the credit card against the lack of an emergency fund that could result in more credit card charges."

"An emergency fund?" Richard asked. "Is that another account?"

Danny laughed. "Actually, emergency funds can accumulate in account three, with your annual expenses. At our next meeting we will discuss emergency funds in greater detail, but for now consider this idea. Split the extra tax savings in three. Put one-third to the credit cards, one-third toward an emergency fund, and one-third toward Richard's trip."

Richard bit his lip. "But that won't be enough to cover it," he said.

"This is just an idea. I've seen this work because you begin building momentum toward all three goals, which motivates you to work harder." Danny explained that by being part of the way toward the trip, it would be easier to get excited to save the rest. The same would be true for the credit cards and emergency fund. "But always remember, my job is to share ideas that I think will work best based on what has worked in the past. Ultimately, you decide what is best for your family."

Richard and Janet were quiet on the ride home—they both had a lot to think about. They didn't know the trouble that was waiting in the mailbox.

Richard's Bad

Richard, wanting to be helpful, started dinner as soon as they'd said goodbye to Marge, who had been taking care of Matthew. Janet put Matthew on one hip to walk outside to get the mail. A moment later, she charged back inside, plunked Matthew into his playpen, and stormed into the kitchen.

"What is this?" Janet demanded, an open envelope in her hand.

"Huh?" Richard said, a spoon poised over the reheated leftovers.

"I think you know exactly what I'm talking about." Janet waved the credit card statement in his face. There, right in black and white for all to see, was a charge for airfare to Montana.

Busted. "I was going to tell you," Richard said sheepishly, like a kid sneaking in after curfew.

"When did you plan on telling me this? We agreed in our meeting with Danny that we were going to save the rest of the money."

"We hadn't had that meeting yet. And I knew with the tax refund that we were so close to what I needed for the trip—"

"You're unbelievable!" Janet was furious. "You had the nerve to make me feel bad about wanting to stay home while all along you had already paid for your plane ticket behind my back?! I thought we committed!"

"This was before that," he tried to explain.

But she wasn't hearing him. All her worst fears came tumbling onto her—Matthew growing up in a home with no parents around, her hating her work forever, Richard getting to do the job he loved—it was too much. "You're not serious about this! You are never going to let me stop working!"

Janet didn't even wait for Richard to respond before she ran from the room and out of the house. She backed out of the garage so fast that the tires squealed when she sped away.

Richard just stood there, spoon in hand, feeling miserable. He knew he should have asked Janet first, but that was when she was talking about divorce anyway. At the time, he'd rationalized that he hadn't taken the trip in a couple years, and he didn't think it was fair he should have to skip it again. So he'd gone ahead.

She didn't come home for hours.

Déjà vu

Richard tried to call Janet over and over on her cell phone but she wouldn't answer. He gave up on dinner and put Matthew to bed, then sat in front of the big screen TV (that they were still paying off), clicking the remote mindlessly. He called her one more time and left a message.

"I know I was wrong, and I'm sorry. I feel awful about what I did. Please call me back," Richard said to her voice mail. He had to stop the message before his voice choked up.

Janet eventually came in, weary, from the garage. She didn't look at him as she put down her purse. But Richard was so glad to see her, he went to hug her. She shrugged him off. Not good.

"I'm sorry," he said. "Where were you?"

"Just wandering around the mall," she said, then glared at him. "Don't worry, I didn't buy anything."

He raised his hands in apology. "Honey, you have every right to be mad. Your goals are so much more important than mine. I promise to be more supportive. And I should never have bought those plane tickets without talking with you about it."

She sighed. "I'm so tired of arguing with you, Richard. This is exactly what we used to do all the time before we started working with Danny."

"I know. We've been doing so much better since we started planning our finances, and we need to stick to it."

Janet laid down a new rule. "From now on we need to agree we won't use our credit cards ever again," she said.

"Totally, it just causes us more headaches than it's worth," Richard said, nodding vigorously.

"What did Danny say? That crazy idea?"

Richard laughed. "You mean about freezing the cards in a cup?"

Janet cracked a smile. "Yeah, that was a funny idea."

"Let's do it!"

While Janet dug around for an old sippy cup of Matthew's, Richard gathered all their cards. Janet even let him go through her wallet. They put them in the cup, filled it with water, sealed it with the plastic lid, and put it in the freezer. They closed the door, and it felt like they were putting their old life behind them.

He tried to put his arm around her, but she backed away. "I'm really worn out," she said. "Good night."

Fundamental #3: Sufficient Liquidity

"How was your week?" Danny asked at their next meeting.

Janet and Richard had been somewhat subdued when they walked in. It had been a rough week for them emotionally, because they still weren't talking things through. But all Janet did was to say quietly, "I got the mail."

Richard looked a bit embarrassed, knowing she meant that night she stormed out. But Danny didn't press it. He launched into Fundamental #3, writing it on their list.

1. Pay off all credit cards and consumer debt

2. Save at least 10% of all your income

3. Maintain sufficient liquidity

"Liquidity?" Richard asked. He was beyond wondering if he'd look stupid asking questions—he wanted to understand everything.

Fundamental #3: Sufficient Liquidity

"Liquidity is when your assets are available to you if you need them, rather than tied up in securities or real estate," Danny said. "It basically means having enough cash on hand for short-term emergencies. Not having enough cash is what will wipe out a family during tough times. And if it doesn't wipe you out, you're likely to end up with a lot of debt trying to stay afloat."

Danny continued, "Before you build up investments in the stock market, real estate, or other more risky investments, you first need to be prepared for the unexpected—but statistically possible—loss of your jobs, major medical bills, real estate crashes, or other risks. Since you both have relatively secure jobs, having a cash emergency reserve of 30% of your annual income would be appropriate."

"That emergency fund," Richard said.

Janet's eyes widened. "That's a whole lot of money."

Danny nodded with understanding. "It is a lot of money, and even contradicts what many financial advisors recommend. Most advisors make a passing recommendation of maintaining an emergency fund of three to six months of living expenses, but rarely do they make it one of the top priorities for their clients. We, however, will make it one of our top priorities."

"Why do you make it so important and other financial advisors don't?" Richard asked.

"To begin with, it's much more interesting for both the advisor and the clients to invest in the stock market. Saving up cash is not nearly as fun as buying stocks or mutual funds, where you can watch the prices go up and down daily in the newspaper. The bigger reality is that most advisors are paid by commissions when you buy or sell stocks and mutual funds, so it's difficult or impossible for them to get paid if you focus on saving up cash."

"That doesn't seem right," Janet said. "An advisor shouldn't recommend buying stock or mutual fund investments before saving up cash, if that is more important at the time."

"I agree with you completely, Janet, which is why it's so important that your relationship with your advisor has as few conflicts of interest as possible."

Danny explained the 30% cash reserve in more detail. That slice of their annual income would be a substantial amount of money and a large percentage of their assets, especially while they're just getting started.

"The best way to accomplish this is by allocating 10% of the savings into a non-retirement account, such as your local bank savings or money market accounts. Then you will invest the remaining 20% in a similar type of account, but held inside of a retirement account such as a 401(k), IRA, or other tax-deferred account."

Danny continued his explanation. "This allows you to use retirement funds, which are usually where the majority of a young family's investments are held, as an emergency fund."

"This is a little confusing to me," Richard asked. "Could you provide an example?"

"Absolutely," Danny responded. "Let's use round numbers to make the math easy. If your family's total annual income were $100,000, then you could save $10,000 in a money market account at your local bank and then save an additional $20,000 in a money market mutual fund that is in your 401(k) retirement plan through your employer."

"Oh, I get it," Richard said. "But what if we had to use that money someday? Aren't there some tax penalties or something like that?"

Janet jumped in. "Yes, I remember our tax guy told me I could never withdraw money early from a retirement account. He said there were huge charges."

"You're both correct," Danny answered. "If, for example, you lost your jobs for six months and had no choice but to use that cash to get by, you would be charged a 10% early penalty from the IRS for the early withdrawal.

"But, if you were in the 37% federal and state tax bracket before you lost your jobs, after being without income for six months, you might then be in the 23% tax bracket because you only had half a year's income. Even after the 10% IRS penalty, you're still below the original 37% tax bracket you were originally in. This allows you to save your emergency fund in your retirement account and not pay taxes on the interest you earn, but the funds are still available in dire circumstances."

"I think I'm beginning to understand this now," Richard said.

"I'm glad to hear that. Are you guys ready to take a little break?" Danny offered, not knowing how much they'd be able to absorb at once.

But understanding a new concept had a relaxing effect on Janet. This money stuff wasn't all that hard. "No, I want to keep going," she said. "We need to stay on track."

Richard's response was wry. "Yeah, it's a little too easy to get off course."

Danny looked from one to the other. "Did something happen?"

"Oh, nothing," Janet said, her tone half joking, half mad. "Richard went and got those hunting trip tickets without asking me."

Richard looked sheepish. "My bad. I had a moment of weakness."

"So," Janet said, "we froze the credit cards."

Danny was puzzled. "You put a hold on them?"

"No," Richard said. "We froze them. In the freezer."

Danny laughed.

Janet added, "We thought it was a good idea. For both of us." A look of understanding passed between them.

"Whatever works for you!" Danny said. "Now let's move on to pensions."

Fundamental #4:
Pensions

"Pensions?" Janet asked, surprised at thinking that long term. "Isn't that a long way off? Who knows—" She was about to say, "Who knows if we'll still be together," but stopped herself. "—Who knows what will happen by then?"

Richard nodded, but for a different reason. "Shouldn't we wait until we have more disposable income and are more established?"

Danny shook his head and added to his piece of paper.

1. Pay off all credit cards and consumer debt

2. Save at least 10% of all your income

3. Maintain sufficient liquidity

4. Fully fund your pensions

"The tax benefits right now of saving money in your employer provided retirement plans are too great to pass up. By contributing in a self-directed pension (retirement plan) such as 401(k), 403(b), IRA or other tax deferred plan, the money you invest becomes a tax deduction now and you don't have to pay taxes on the money until you withdraw it."

"Every year somebody tries to get me to put money into those accounts," Janet admitted, "but we never had the money at tax time, so I ignored them."

"Something I learned long ago," Danny said, "is that waiting until tax time to invest in retirement accounts means it rarely happens. If you don't plan ahead for it, there usually isn't any money left over when you're filing. That's why investing in your employer-provided plan is best because the money can be automatically deducted little by little from each paycheck before you even see it. This makes sure the money gets invested before you have a chance to spend it. Sometimes employers even provide matching funds, which is free money. You should get as much of that as you can."

Richard was beginning to wonder how all of this was going to add up. "Wait a minute, Danny. If we're saving because of Fundamentals #2 and #3, and now you're adding this to it, where are we supposed to get all of this money?"

"Keep in mind that the money you contribute to these plans counts towards the 10% savings we talked about in Fundamental #2," Danny said. "Depending on tax laws, it's possible that by fully funding your pension plan, you may exceed the 10% or it may become more than you can afford. But you can always adjust it. Aim for at least 10% of your income. If you can comfortably afford more, try to fully fund your pension. You'll be thankful you did."

"What happens if—" Janet started, then stopped.

"If what?" Danny asked.

Janet chewed her lip. "If sometime, you know, we split up."

Richard's eyes roamed the backyard, his lips tightening. But he waited for Danny's answer. It would be good to know.

"Well," Danny said slowly, "it depends on whatever settlement you decide on at that time. It could be that whatever amount was saved by each of you in your names would revert to you, or that you'd take the total and split it, like everything else. But saving for retirement is something you need to do whether you're married or single."

Janet felt bad she'd brought it up. She shook her head to clear it. "Sorry, I was just curious." She changed the subject. "Would that insurance investment my uncle suggested count toward this?"

Danny appeared to be wiping a dubious look off his face. "For the majority of people, insurance products with an investment feature attached are—well, they're not what they're cracked up to be."

"Really?" Richard said, glad someone else could be the bad guy. "Uncle Roger made it sound like the Holy Grail of retirement plans."

"The best way to view insurance is for what it was designed for, and that is insurance against sudden loss," Danny explained. "This includes a fire in your home, a major auto accident, or a death. Insurance should not be considered an investment."

Janet frowned. "I understand what you mean with the house and car, but what do you mean for a death?"

"Life insurance should be used to replace income for dependants if there is an unexpected death. In your case, if one of you were to pass away, the remaining spouse and baby depend on your income to make ends meet. But even a stay-at-home mom may need life insurance, because if she were to pass away, the husband would have to hire a childcare provider so he could continue to work."

Janet became grim. Her husband was a police officer, after all. "I think we need more insurance. But what about the investment part?"

"Those insurance policies that accumulate a cash value usually tend to be overpriced, poor investments."

"What do you mean they are overpriced?" Richard asked.

"The hidden expenses in those policies are usually outrageously expensive. With a very few exceptions, you can usually get a lot more insurance for far less cost, and then invest the rest of the money in better investments that are made for that purpose."

Richard was nodding. "I think there's a plan for that at work, but I'm not sure I'm signed up for it. There's the union plan, of course, but I could do more."

Danny gathered up the papers on the table. "We've covered a lot today. Before next time, why don't you both look into the pension plans at work, along with any insurance opportunities? That way we can maximize it as much as possible. Next meeting we'll cover Fundamental #5."

Janet groaned. "Is it hard?"

Danny smiled. "No, but it's what most people have the strongest feelings about—what size mortgage to get."

Mr. Nice Guy

On the way home, Richard tried to break the ice.

"That wasn't too bad," he said. "I think we're getting the hang of it."

"Yeah, but next is mortgages," Janet said. "I'm not looking forward to that." It didn't help that their route home always took them right past Stephanie's place. Every time Janet drove past it, she wondered if they would ever have a home that nice. "Isn't it weird to you that Danny has such a modest house?" she said. "If he's so good with money, he should have a fancier place."

"You mean like some McMansion?" Richard said. "I don't think his house is modest. It's classy. I'm sure he could afford any house he wants."

"Maybe." Janet stared out the window as they drove.

Richard cleared his throat. "I'm also thinking about something else," he said.

Janet turned to him curiously.

"I got a good offer for the motorcycle." Richard's eyes stayed on the road. "We can get rid of that payment at least."

Janet's jaw dropped. "Oh, honey—" She knew how he loved that bike.

He shrugged it off. "I can always get another one, when the time is right."

* * *

In the coming days Janet and Richard both talked with their respective benefits departments about insurance, pensions, and retirement funds. There were a lot of opportunities they'd not been taking advantage of. Janet found out that her company provided matching funds for a 401(k)— that "free money" Danny talked about. Richard's pension had already been accumulating, so they weren't at the zero he thought they were. He had his police pension and also a 457 retirement plan he didn't even know about. Apparently when he was first hired, the HR department had set him up to automatically deduct 2.5% of his paychecks for retirement. And, he could augment that with further contributions.

He'd never put Janet on his life insurance forms, however, which was stupid. Now, as he filled out the forms to add her and Matthew as beneficiaries, he felt a twinge that if things kept being so topsy-turvy with their relationship, she might not be on the policy that long. But, he would protect her while he could.

That night, he stopped to get some of Janet's favorite Thai takeout on the way home.

"Ta-da!" he said, opening the bags in the kitchen.

"That smells great!" Janet said, Matthew on her hip. "We haven't eaten out in so long." Then she had a moment of suspicion. "Wait a minute—you didn't use a credit card, did you?"

Richard shook his head. "Nope, they're still frozen. This is out of my cash for this week. So you don't have to cook."

Janet looked so surprised that Richard felt a little goofy about it. He got out the plates and started dishing up the Pad Thai, trying not to look at her.

He used his cash for this week? Janet was touched. "Well, honey, what I mean is..." she said, "...that was nice of you." Then she said the magic words. "Thank you."

Richard grinned into the carton.

Fundamental #5: Mortgage

Danny saved the mortgage fundamental for last. He explained that for most Americans, their home is the largest and best investment they will ever make. This isn't only because of the long-term historical appreciation of real estate and the tax advantages, but also because of the lifestyle benefits that home ownership provides.

With that, Danny returned to his paper and wrote the final fundamental on the list:

1. Pay off all credit cards and consumer debt

2. Save at least 10% of all your income

3. Maintain sufficient liquidity

4. Fully fund your pensions

5. Have the right sized house and mortgage

"Picking your house is an important decision on many different levels, but from the financial perspective there are a few formulas. A rough figure is to buy a home that's worth 2 to 2½ times your gross annual income."

Janet did the math in her head and frowned. "But when we asked that real estate agent, she said we could afford a lot more than that."

"Hm," Danny said, sounding mildly disapproving. "She said you could qualify for a larger loan. That doesn't necessarily mean you can actually afford it. Remember it's in the best interests of the mortgage company to get you to borrow as much as possible. They don't take into consideration what other financial obligations or goals you might have. Their mindset is that all your money should go to the house."

"But we've learned already we need to do a lot more with our money," Richard said.

"Right. Based on your combined income at the moment, the estimated price you're looking at is..." Danny wrote down a number that was 2½ times their income. "That gives you a rough starting point, although in markets like California or New York, the realities might be different."

Janet was discouraged. "That's way less than I thought it would be. What can we get for that amount?"

"You can get what's appropriate for you right now, without having to stretch or neglect other financial needs," Danny said. "Remember, you've just started a family. Now is not the time to overextend, but it's also not the time to have too little."

"You mean to keep renting," Richard said. "My dad always rented—he says that's good enough for him."

"Where does he live now?" Danny asked.

"In a one-bedroom apartment on the edge of town," Richard admitted. "It's been that way since he and Mom divorced."

"Not that that's bad," Danny said. "You just have to ask yourself if that's what you want."

Janet was already shaking her head when Richard said, "It's not. But what about a down payment?"

"That's just the direction I was heading," Danny answered. "You want to maintain a mortgage that is at least 50% or more of the value of the home so you can take advantage of the benefits of leverage. As the value of your earnings and your home increases, at some point the value of your home will be equal to 100% or 125% of your annual income. If you're still earning income and need a larger house, trading up may be a good option."

Janet wanted to make sure she understood. "So, just to use simple numbers, if our annual income was $100,000 and rose to $200,000, then selling our $250,000 home and buying one worth $400,000 might be a good idea?"

"That's right," Danny nodded. "But there are also many emotional factors to consider, such as if you even want or need a different house. Maybe you want a larger home as your family grows or you'd prefer to live in another neighborhood. These things are important to consider in addition to the financial side."

"But if we keep trading up, we will never pay it off. Why shouldn't we buy one house and pay it off?" Richard asked.

"Most people have a psychological aversion to carrying a mortgage and dream of a paid-off home in retirement. So your question is a very good one, Richard." Danny explained in more detail. "There are a lot of people who make extra payments to their mortgage, often before making retirement contributions or even paying off credit cards. This is a huge mistake for many reasons, some of what we've already discussed and for other reasons as well."

"That's the leverage you're talking about," Janet said.

"Right," Danny said. "Where did you learn about that?"

"My dad talks about it all the time."

"That he does," Richard agreed drily.

"Hey," Janet said, swatting at him a little. "If there's one thing Dad knows about, it's money. From what I remember, leverage allows your investment to grow at a much higher rate than without leverage. It was a little confusing, but I think I can explain it with an example better."

"Please do, Janet," Danny said encouraging her.

"If we were to buy a $100,000 house with a $20,000 down payment, and the house increases in value by 4% at the end of the first year, it will be worth $104,000. That's a $4,000 gain on your $20,000 investment. So it's really a 20% gain on the $20,000, instead of only a 4% gain on the total house value. I think that is it," Janet said with a little uncertainty.

"That's it exactly, Janet." Danny said. "By using leveraged (which is a fancy way of saying 'borrowed') money, you're able to earn the investment gains you would with a $100,000 investment, but you only have to invest $20,000."

"Oh, that makes sense!" Richard said suddenly. It was like a light bulb went off over his head. "That's cool."

"What you don't want to do," Danny cautioned, "is tie up too much of your money into an asset you can't liquidate quickly, such as a house. If you've heard the phrase, 'House rich, cash poor,' that's what it means. Having a lump sum of cash and carrying a mortgage gives you more options and security than having no cash, but a paid-off home. However, a too-expensive home will eat into your lifestyle in other ways that are important to you, not to mention erode your ability to save and develop other assets."

Janet still wasn't entirely happy. "Danny, what about this? I have this friend who doesn't even work, and her husband bought them this huge, new place. How come she can afford that and we have to start so small? She seems to have tons of money, all the time."

Danny shrugged. "It could be that her husband simply rakes in the big bucks. But it could also be a house of cards. If they haven't built a strong foundation—financially, I mean—it could blow over."

"Maybe," Janet said. She wondered if she should stop letting Stephanie always pay for lunch.

On the Hunt

Danny had walked them through the Five Fundamentals, and now it was time to get used to thinking that way. Janet and Richard didn't have another appointment with Danny for about a month—but it was a very busy month.

Richard finally got to go on his hunting trip. After all, they couldn't waste those plane tickets. Janet didn't make a big deal out of his going like she had other years. There was no "call me when you get there" or "I'll miss you" coming out of her mouth. But when she dropped him at the airport to meet his buddies and drove away with only Matthew in the car seat, she couldn't help but feel a bit lonely.

He was gone for a week that September. For an entire week, Janet had to juggle babysitting, housework, cooking, mail—everything—not to mention still trying to meet with clients and make sales. It was one of the toughest weeks of her life.

Richard, in the meantime, had gone off on his trip acting as though he were all set to have a great time, but in the back of his mind was the constant wondering of how things would be when he got back. Maybe she wouldn't miss him. Maybe she'd be fine without him. But he knew one thing—he'd have to find out one way or the other which way their marriage was going, and soon. It was driving him crazy.

There was no chance to talk about it when he flew back in, though. When Janet picked him up, she had something looming on her mind— Matthew's first birthday party.

"Everybody has these huge parties around here," Janet said as she drove. "Mom wants us to get a special cake and a clown."

"A clown? That'll just scare him." Richard reached to tickle Matthew in the backseat. "Just because everyone else blows a ton of money on their one-year-olds, doesn't mean we have to."

Janet nodded, a frown still creasing her forehead. Richard tried not to stare—she always looked pretty that way. He didn't know if she had missed him, but he sure was missing her.

"I was thinking the same thing," Janet said. "Maybe something simple is better."

"Yeah, just some family and a couple friends—not Stephanie."

Janet laughed. Now she looked even prettier.

* * *

The party was a huge success, probably because it wasn't huge. Family, a few neighbors, and some friends, some hotdogs on the grill, a cake Janet and Richard made together (lopsided but tasted good), and plenty of presents to surround Matthew with wrapping paper.

Richard did everything he could to be a great host, joking with the other fathers who didn't know why they were there and making the ladies feel at home. But Janet saw how her little house filled up with all those people, and could only think again about wanting a larger place. Why couldn't they raise Matthew in a house like Stephanie's?

That night, when they were tucking a very sleepy little boy into bed, Richard congratulated Janet on a great party.

"I think that went well," he said. "Nice job, honey."

"Yeah, it was okay," she said.

"Everyone had a great time—especially Matthew."

"But it was all so crowded," Janet said. "There's not enough room here."

Richard deflated a little. He knew she was tired, but it was discouraging to hear her still longing for a house they couldn't afford. "We'll get there. Danny said—"

"Danny said, Danny said, Danny said!" Janet lit into him. "Maybe he doesn't know everything."

Richard stuck out his chin. "He's been right so far."

Janet knew she wasn't being fair. "It just feels like it's taking forever to get where we want to be."

"I know." Richard reached out to hug her, but she pulled away.

"I'm exhausted," she said, and she went into the bedroom without him.

Asset Allocation

Janet and Richard's next meeting with Danny would cap off the "educational" part of their working together. They had all their fundamentals established, were on their way to getting out of consumer debt, and knew what saving and pensions looked like on a month-to-month basis. Janet just wished everything wasn't taking so long.

"All we need to do now," Danny said, "is tackle asset allocation. Most investors, and also financial professionals, tend to overcomplicate asset allocation."

"I might, too, if I knew what it meant," Richard joked. Janet gave a small smile.

Danny chuckled. "It's just a fancy way of saying how your money should be divided among different types of investments. It gets overcomplicated for a few reasons. There has been a lot of research on what is the best mix of stocks, bonds, and cash, and the majority of financial professionals follow these studies. But much of this research was designed to work with the large amounts of money in pension funds and does not work as well for the average American who doesn't have billions of dollars to invest. But even those in academia are questioning the industry norms because of some recent research, and more importantly, because of the real world events of the most recent recession."

"The other factor that is somewhat ignored by the large instructional investors, is the fact that a family's personal residence often makes up the majority of their financial assets. Given the value, potential growth, and the tax benefits of real estate, it's a mistake to pretend your residence is not part of the equation."

"For that to apply to us," Janet said, "we'd have to buy a house."

"It'll come, honey," Richard said.

Danny explained the basic framework of dividing assets equally into three classes: equity investments in businesses, real estate, and interest-earning assets.

Equities

Danny started with equities, "Within this framework, one-third of all of assets are invested in equities, including any small businesses you own, individual stocks, or mutual funds that own stock in companies. For most people, it isn't possible to own enough different individual company stocks to be safely diversified."

"I remember that one," Richard said. "Don't put all of your eggs in one basket."

"That's correct." Danny added, "In order to keep a properly diversified portfolio of stocks, the average family should invest in mutual funds. You can think of these as a basket of many different companies' stock, and you only buy a portion of the companies that are owned by the mutual fund. For example, one mutual fund can own stock in 500 different companies. You may be one of thousands of investors investing in the same mutual fund."

"The mutual fund uses all of the money invested by you and other investors to purchase stock in many different companies. The benefit of this is that when a few companies decline in value, some may stay the same, and others will grow. By owning so many companies in one mutual fund, on average, hopefully the fund increases in value even though there were some individual losses."

Real Estate

Next was real estate. "For asset allocation," Danny said, "we only measure the equity you own in real estate. Do you guys understand the term 'equity'?"

Janet, who had a good grasp of real estate, said, "Equity is the value that would be left over if someone sells their home and pays off the mortgage."

"That's it. For our purposes, in addition to your personal residence, we also include any vacation homes, investment real estate, or vacant land." Danny continued, "You could also include REITs which are real estate investment trusts similar to mutual funds, but they only invest in real estate."

"So that's a third of our investments in company stocks, and a third in real estate," Richard said. "Where do we invest the final third?"

Interest-Earning

"In anything that earns interest. Within this third you can include your bank savings account, money market funds, certificates of deposit (or CDs), and bonds."

"You know, I've never understood what a bond is," Janet said.

"Now is a perfect time to cover that," Danny answered. "The easiest way to understand the difference between a stock and bond is to imagine a friend who wants to start a small business. In order to get the business started, he needs start-up money for a lease, equipment, payroll, etc.

"He might have some money, but not enough to get it started on his own, so he approaches all of his friends and family as investors in his new company. He has two ways he can propose that you invest. He may offer to sell you stocks, bonds, or both."

"This is what your sister wanted us to do last Thanksgiving, Richard," Janet said.

"Yes, but thank goodness we didn't invest in her company," he replied.

"Why is that?" Danny asked.

"Well," Janet explained, "she always has a different scheme or investment idea. She wanted us to give her the money she'd need to start a crafts business, and offered us 10% ownership."

"It sounds like she wanted to sell you stock in that company, so you would essentially have become a part owner in the company." Danny decided to use the sister's company as an example to continue explaining stocks and bonds. "If she needed $10,000 total for example, she may sell

10 stocks for $1,000 each. If you invested $2,000, you would have received 20% ownership in the company."

"Hm," Janet said. "She wanted us to front the entire $2,000 she needed, but was only offering 10% ownership."

Danny shook his head. "That, my friends, probably wouldn't be the best deal for you. If you put up all the money, you'd usually want to own more than 10% of the company. "

Richard winced. "That wouldn't have worked."

"But she'd be doing all the work," Janet said.

"But you're taking all the risk, financially anyway. So you should probably get a larger share of the benefits of any increase in value, because you're risking losing it all if it doesn't fly."

"Which it didn't," Richard admitted. "She's totally onto something else now."

"How do bonds work?" Janet asked.

"Instead of selling stock, a small business owner might instead offer to sell bonds. Bonds are financial agreements where, unlike stock, the terms are predetermined. If your sister in our example still needed the $2,000, she might offer bonds that pay 10% interest every year for a fixed amount of years. So regardless of how well or poorly the company does, the bond guarantees you $200 in income each year, assuming the company stays in business and has enough money to make the payment. And at the end of the term of the bond, you get your original investment back."

"So it's kind of like a certificate of deposit from a bank?" Janet asked.

"Well, kind of, but bonds can be bought and sold on the market, and their prices can rise and fall depending on interest rates," Danny said. "Bonds are often viewed as less risky than equities because the amount of money you will earn with them is predetermined. Also, bond holders are legally supposed to be paid before stock holders in most circumstances, so if a company goes under, bond holders are usually in a safer position than stock holders. You also get the principal back. But bonds, like all investments, have risks too, and in the right circumstances can be just as, or more risky, than stocks."

Danny reviewed the investment options in their retirement plans and gave them investment recommendations based on his asset allocation plan. Janet and Richard left that meeting with a clearer understanding of how stocks, bonds, and asset allocation all worked together. Their meetings with Danny would now be on a more "check in" basis, about once every three months.

On the way home, they discussed how far they'd come.

"It all makes sense now," Richard said. "I'm not afraid of money anymore."

Janet nodded. "Me, too. I can't believe now that we were even surviving as we were. It was like driving without a license. Everyone should know these things."

"The country would be in a lot better shape, that's for sure."

"I still wish, though—" Janet hesitated.

"What?" Richard asked, already knowing what she was going to say.

"Well, that the money 'rules' would let us get a more expensive house. I'm not sure I like that part—"

But she cut herself off as they turned a corner. There, right in front of them, was Stephanie's house, with a large "foreclosure" sign out front.

"I can't believe it!" Janet exclaimed. "She's losing her house?"

"Maybe it was a house of cards, like Danny said." Richard reached for Janet's hand. "That will never happen to us."

Janet bit her lip. She knew Richard was right, but she still didn't know how she felt about their marriage. If Richard was always at work and she couldn't be home to raise her child, what was the point?

Then came the moment of truth.

The Chase

Richard had to work the next evening on a late night surveillance with the narcotics team. Even in his new role as supervisor, he still worked side by side with his team.

Tonight he was partnered in an unmarked car with Jay, a long time colleague, in the driver's seat. They were expecting to serve a search warrant as soon as a shipment of methamphetamine was delivered to a house by a Columbian they had been following for the past eight months.

Usually they wore casual clothes with just their badge and gun concealed under their shirts, but tonight they dressed up in their "raid" gear. They still wore blue jeans, but they wore a bullet proof vest covered in pockets to hold handcuffs, radio, spare bullets, and each team member carried an extra handgun in their vest.

It took a while for things to get rolling. Their target wasn't showing up, so when Janet called his cell phone, Richard picked up. He seldom talked with her when he was on duty, but this time he and Jay were just staring into space, waiting.

"Richard—" she started, and he could tell by her voice she was stressed. "When are you coming home?"

"Why, what do you need?"

"You said we'd have takeout tonight."

Richard winced. "Oh, honey, I forgot. This case came up and I'm on surveillance. I won't be home until late." He knew if she could see him in his raid gear, she'd stress out even more.

"What?" she said, her voice rising. "Why didn't you tell me?"

Richard was about to reply when he saw movement down the street. "Is that the car?" he asked Jay, pointing to the sedan creeping up the street.

"Who are you talking to?" Janet asked.

"One sec, honey." He became intent as Jay pulled out his binoculars to try to read the license plate.

"I think that may be our guy," Jay said.

Janet said over the phone, "What's going on?"

A voice came over their police radio from one of the other surveillance teams. "Units standby, suspect is northbound on Crenshaw toward the primary location."

The sedan rolled slowly past the house—and pulled up within twenty yards of where Richard and Jay were parked. The driver looked into their undercover car and made eye contact with Jay, who was sitting reclined far behind the steering wheel.

"That's the Columbian," Richard said.

Suddenly the sedan's wheels peeled out.

"Oh no!" Jay said. "He's running!" He picked up the police radio. "We've been made. Suspect is fleeing northbound on Crenshaw and we're in pursuit."

The Chase

"Gotta go, honey!" Richard said. "Will call you later!"
He disconnected just as she was saying, "Be careful!"

Tense Waiting

Janet paced at home, unable to relax or fall asleep, as many cops' wives often do. Richard was chasing some dirtbag, and she couldn't rest until she knew he was safe again.

And all I could do was nag him about takeout, she thought. *This is why he never tells me about work.*

As hours passed, her anxiety got the better of her. She wandered their home, looking at photos and remembering all the vacations and family events when the photos had been taken. Seeing Matthew sleeping peacefully in the crib she and Richard had purchased together, her heart filled with love.

And that's when she realized that worrying about money wasn't worth losing her marriage. In her moment of panic she became determined to do anything to keep her family together and to make this marriage work. She was with the right guy, and she wasn't going to lose him.

Come on, Richard, she thought. *Call me.*

On Foot

"You ou better not let him get away from you!" Richard yelled from the passenger seat as his adrenalin started pumping.

"You just get on the radio and call for a black and white and leave the driving to me!" Jay snapped back.

"Suspect is eastbound on Main Street," Richard yelled into the radio. He knew he was yelling, but was trying to calm himself down.

"I can't believe he missed that oncoming car!" Jay yelled. "Damn that was close!"

The sedan was driving so recklessly, he had nearly crashed three times in the four blocks they had been chasing it.

"He's not going to make..." Before Jay could finish his sentence, the sedan crashed into a parked car. Jay had just enough time to brake before crashing into the sedan himself.

Richard yelled, "Suspect crashed. Running eastbound on Main Street toward Oxnard Boulevard." Richard threw the microphone on the floorboard. He had the passenger door open and was starting to run after the suspect before Jay could get their car to a complete stop.

It had been a long time since Richard had chased anyone on foot.

He was running with everything he had in him, over lawns and through backyards. He saw the suspect enter the door of a nondescript house.

Without hesitating, Richard pulled his gun out with his right hand and kicked the door in with his left leg. The house was pitch black until Richard flicked on the light at the end of his handgun.

As soon as the light came on, he saw the suspect hiding behind a couch with that familiar deer in the headlights look on his face. "Put your hands up!" Richard demanded.

The suspect was cornered between a wall and Richard, who was the only thing between him and the door. The suspect jumped out from behind the couch and charged for the door.

Richard's high school wrestling days were instinctively coming back to him as he jumped the guy. The two of them struggled on the ground for a few seconds, until Richard managed to get him in handcuffs.

"Are you okay?" Jay asked as he ran into the house.

"What the hell took you so long?" Richard asked, trying to catch his breath.

"Well, if you would have told us what house you were trying to break into all alone like you were Batman or something, maybe we would have found you faster!" Jay teased him.

When Richard got home that night, Janet's hug was tight.

Getting Lucky

The weeks slid by with Janet and Richard making strong progress toward their financial goals. One night, Richard brought flowers home. He swept Janet up into his arms.

"Time to celebrate!" he said. "Let's go out tonight."

"What are we celebrating?" Janet asked, laughing. She'd been much more affectionate since the night of Richard's chase, and they were back to hugging whenever they could.

"I checked online, and we just made the last automatic payment on the last credit card!" He twirled her around. "And tonight, I want time with my wife. I've already called your folks, we can drop Matthew off on the way."

"On the way where?"

"It's a surprise."

* * *

Next thing Janet knew, they were pulling up to the restaurant where they'd had their first anniversary.

When the waiter checked in at their table, he asked if they'd like to start with something to drink.

Without a moment's hesitation, Janet said, "Champagne please."

"Absolutely ma'am," the waiter replied, "And for you sir?"

"No, bring us a whole bottle!" Janet answered for him with a big smile directed at Richard.

After the waiter walked away, Richard smiled and said, "It's been a while since we've been able to have an entire bottle."

"Yes, but the difference is now we know exactly where the money is coming from."

"That bottle used to lead to a pretty good evening for me," Richard said.

"Well, tonight just might, too," Janet hinted with a grin.

They had a great dinner, and after finishing their second bottle of champagne, they both agreed there was no way they could drive. They went for a walk on the beach. It was deserted because it had gotten pretty late.

Janet had been flirting with Richard all evening at the restaurant, and now, after the champagne, almost all of her inhibitions were gone. Richard wasn't feeling much different. When they walked around a rocky cove on the dark, deserted beach, Richard pulled Janet to him and began kissing her like they hadn't in years.

Soon they were at it like a couple of high-school kids at the drive-in. Richard got a little carried away and started unbuttoning her shirt.

Breathless and laughing, Janet said, "What if someone sees us?"

"Do you really care right now?" Richard asked.

"No...not really!"

* * *

Later, Richard and Janet, a bit disheveled, were back in the car, driving home. Janet hummed as she gazed out the window, happy. Richard took his eyes off the road for a moment to look at her.

"That was fun," he said.

She nodded, her eyes sparkling.

"I think things are going pretty good between us now."

Janet was surprised. "What do you mean?"

"Well, things were rough for a while, now they seem good." He had his eyes back on the road.

She reached for his arm and gave it a squeeze. "Very good."

He cleared his throat. "Can I ask you something?"

"Sure, honey."

"No more divorce lawyer?"

Janet's face dropped. "Oh, Richard! No, no more divorce lawyer." She hadn't thought about it for ages.

"Good." He took her hand in his.

Janet chuckled. "You remember, that was just before we started with Danny. Did I ever tell you the lawyer had recommended him to me also? Before you even got us started on that application. I think she knew our problems were mostly about money, and if we solved them, we'd be in good shape."

Richard nodded. "I think she was right!"

Fast Forward

Gradually everything Danny had taught Janet and Richard about money became second nature to them. Their spending and saving habits had changed for the better, and they could have fun when they wanted to. By Janet and Richard's fourth anniversary, everything was just about perfect.

Janet and Richard were still meeting with Danny a few times a year. Their life looked completely different than when they first met with him.

First, and most importantly, they had a three-month old little girl named Elizabeth. But with this baby, they had time to prepare. Through a goal-setting exercise in their sessions with Danny, Janet had been able to stop working right about the time Elizabeth was born. They'd achieved as a family their number one financial goal.

Two years later, Janet was still no longer working and neither she nor Richard was even slightly worried about their income. Their credit cards stayed paid off, in full, every month, and they'd even purchased a nice starter home to raise their family. Every year Richard was able to go on his hunting trip because they planned ahead and automatically saved for it in the same account they used to pay their annual car insurance bill.

Fast Forward

Their little system worked almost on autopilot with occasional check-ins with Danny to adjust their taxes or rebalance their investments. Most importantly, Richard was actually working less and spending more time at home with Janet and the kids.

Now, Janet and Richard send Danny a family photo every year as he had become a part of their extended—and solvent—family.

A Word from Chuck

As I was wrapping up this book, there were many things I wanted to include. I finally had to accept I couldn't cover everything. In fact, I removed several chapters while editing because, although the information was important, I realized I had strayed from my original intent with this book.

The majority of upper-middle income America has similar financial struggles as Richard and Janet, which revolve around the emotional aspects of money. Usually, to borrow Pareto's Principle, 80% of the solution will come from only 20% of the effort. In other words, you will notice the greatest improvements in your life by improving the 20% of areas that account 80% of the problems.

In order to stay true to that theory, the purpose of this book is to bring to your attention to the financial issues that cause the most stress and anxiety and give you the few tools that will most likely lead to the solution.

With that in mind, this book is not complete. No single book on personal finance can ever be complete without spanning hundreds of volumes. There are many topics I had to gloss over in order to keep the book entertaining and moving forward. For many people, this book will be their very first introduction to personal finance. It's written as a novel specifically for that audience.

A subject that is equally important, but not included in detail in this book, is a review of your insurance policies—home, auto, life, health, and umbrella policies. Most insurance advice is provided by people selling insurance, so you always have to question if their advice is in your best interests, or that of the salesperson.

Another area not covered is estate planning. Many of middle-income America feels that estate planning is for "rich people." Nothing can be further from the truth. If you have people you care about, particularly a spouse and kids, making sure they are provided for concerns people of all income levels.

Even more important are family value choices such as who will gain custody of your children if something were to happen to you. It's easy to push these concerns aside because of more pressing issues, but there's no greater peace of mind than knowing your family is protected.

Experienced investors will have quickly recognized my overly simplified explanation of asset allocation toward the end of the book. Asset allocation is important to balance the risk of investing across several different investment types, while still providing the opportunity to earn higher investment returns to keep ahead of inflation. But as your investment portfolio grows, so will the need to expand and make it more complicated, while improving diversity, safety, and growth potential.

Within each of the three asset classes discussed, each can and often should be further diversified. For example, real estate can be divided further into your primary residence, secondary or vacation home, investment property such as rental homes, apartments, and commercial property, and finally vacant land.

Interest-earning assets can also be further divided. After your initial investment in cash for your emergency fund, your options include money market mutual funds, certificates of deposit (CDs) of varying maturity lengths, short-, medium- and long-term bonds, and mutual funds that invest in many of these types of assets.

Finally, equity in business can be purchased in just as many formats. The foundation of your assets should usually be in a broad based large cap U.S. equity index fund. This is a low-cost mutual fund that purchases shares in hundreds of large U.S. based companies.

Eventually you need to diversify beyond large U.S. companies and consider mutual funds that invest in international firms and small, medium and large companies. As your investment portfolio expands, you may consider individual company stocks, which may include your employer's company stock or direct investment in your own small business or that of another.

These more complex assets have been the subject of many books, but these investments often are not ideal, or necessary, for people getting started. You can quickly diversify your interest earning funds into bonds and your equity assets into small company or international stock mutual funds, once you've established the foundation.

The key point, and also a big mistake many families make, is that investing in the more complex assets should only happen after establishing a foundation in all three categories of the basic asset allocation section.

People get themselves in trouble, for example, by buying rental property before having a fully funded emergency fund. As soon as their property doesn't have a renter, they can quickly eat up cash making the mortgage payments while it's vacant.

The same thing happens if they invest in risky business investments without having an emergency fund established. Self employed people are prone to investing all of their earnings back into their businesses. This is important and often necessary for the entrepreneur's success, but it's risky. Their logic is that money invested in their company will earn far more money than in the stock or bond market. That is often true, but ignores the whole point. The purpose of proper asset allocation is not to find the highest earning investments as much as it is to spread your risk across several investments so when one crashes, which often happens, you still have assets elsewhere that are doing well.

A final note is that I've attempted to describe a simple framework that will work for most people, but nothing is ever "one size fits all." Each of the rules in the Five Fundamentals and asset allocation needs to be customized for each family's unique situation.

The factors that are important to consider are risk factors such as security of employment or self-employment, age, health, and time before retirement.

These risk factors are what I use to determine the appropriate asset allocations between the many different interest earning, stock market, and real estate investments. I also use these factors to increase or decrease the size of the emergency fund. Higher risk people, such as self-employed, often have greater fluctuations in cash flow and thus a larger emergency fund is appropriate.

For those looking for the next level, there are two paths you can take. The first is to continue your self-guided education through books, seminars, and coaching. The second is to work directly with a financial advisor who can cater to your unique needs.

I highly recommend you seek the advice of a Fee-Only financial advisor. An excellent place to begin your search is at www.acaplanners.org or www.napfa.org. **And last, but certainly not least, meet and connect with me online and receive more in-depth FREE training at www.ChuckRylant.com.**

Bonus Material

The book that you hold in your hands is only the beginning. There is a ton of FREE training available only to readers of this book. Using passwords hidden in this book, you can access some very powerful training that will take you and your finances to the next level.

Visit: www.NoMoreMoneyWorry.com

About the Author

*C*huck J. Rylant is a CERTIFIED FINANCIAL PLANNER™ that works one-on-one with clients like those depicted in this story. He stumbled into this industry after years of living in the "Rat Race." He was born into poverty and spent the first sixteen years of his life raised on welfare and in government housing.

At the ripe old age of eighteen, Chuck made his first investment of his hard earned $1,000 in a mutual fund that was a completely inappropriate, but an easy sale for a commissioned stockbroker, or otherwise said a salesperson.

Years later, through lots of self-guided education and even more mistakes in the market, Chuck figured out how money and investing really works. He eventually earned the formal education and financial planning credentials, an MBA degree, and tax training to be "qualified" to give personal financial planning advice.

It wasn't until Chuck had a wife, divorce, remarriage, stepchild, businesses, jobs, his own child, a deceased parent, and worked as a financial advisor with other real-world complicated families, that he discovered what really mattered about money and happiness.

About the Author

Chuck's experiences leading up to this book have been wide and far reaching. Chuck has been a SWAT team member, auto mechanic, police detective, welder, financial advisor and owner of multiple businesses.

Through these experiences and his lifelong study of personal finance, Chuck has discovered how to design his lifestyle so he spends more time with his family doing the things he loves. Chuck travels extensively and often spends months at a time with his family in places like Brazil, Columbia, Mexico, Costa Rica, China, and others.

Chuck is married and has two children. They live near the beach in California where he has a consulting company providing group and private coaching to families and small business owners so they can live extraordinary lives.

Chuck rarely takes on new private clients, but occasionally accepts those he finds interesting. To learn more about what he is up to and get more in-depth FREE training, **visit his blog at <ins>www.ChuckRylant.com</ins>**.

Acknowledgments

There are many who enabled me to do the many things I've been fortunate to do. There were also many who've come and gone during my almost four decade journey where I've learned the subtleties contained in this book.

There is no way I can name all of you individually, because I would certainly leave someone off the list. But here is the short list.

First, I thank my wife, Heather, for tolerating and supporting this and all of my other "ideas," some of which have been better than others.

To my clients, who have trusted me to share with you what I know and allowed me learn from you as well.

To Laura Mathews, my amazing editor from whom I learned a great deal during this project. This story would not have worked without her talent.

To my friends, family, and colleagues, who agreed to read, critique, edit, and gently straighten me out. You know who you are.

I have to give credit to Bert Whitehead, who enabled me, through his teachings, to take my vast and disorganized knowledge of personal finance and organize it into the system I now use, teach, and is deeply woven throughout this book.

Acknowledgments

To the many colleges at the Alliance of Cambridge Advisors (ACA), whom I have to equally credit for helping me learn this way of holistic personal financial planning.

And finally, to my colleagues at the National Association of Personal Financial Advisors (NAPFA) for showing me that there was an ethical way to serve clients through Fee-Only financial planning.

Made in the USA
San Bernardino, CA
10 March 2017